The Xia Stories — Once In A Lifetime

ISBN: 978-1-951742-48-5   [Paperback Edition]
        978-1-951742-49-2   [eBook Edition]

Printed and bound in The United States of America.

Published by

The Mulberry Books, LLC.
8330 E Quincy Avenue,
Denver CO 80237

themulberrybooks.com

THE XIA STORIES

Once In A Lifetime

BONNIE SHAO

To my family and friends,
for all their love and support.

Table of Contents

Luolan and her Chinese friends and family speak Mandarin Chinese. When Luolan is at home or in China, most of the time she and her Chinese friends and family are speaking Mandarin, although the words are in English. There is a glossary at the back for all the Chinese words if you don't understand them. Enjoy the story!

Big News

My story starts with the day Mama told us that we were moving. It wasn't just down the street to the newly built neighborhood. It was across the world. To a country I hadn't really thought about much in my life.

It was Monday. Now, I know you're probably all thinking, *Bleh, end of the weekend and the start of evil school, yuck,* but honestly, I don't get how school is so bad. I mean, yeah, my teacher's really strict and she yells at the class a lot, but other than that, school's fine.

I even like to take tests!

But my brother, Lizhong, is a whole other story. I guess that's because he's worried about the *Gao Kao,* this really big test you take in twelfth grade to get into college. He's in sixth grade (going into seventh next year) and he's seriously stressed about it even though he has five years to prepare. Very paranoid about grades, my brother. I call Lizhong Ge Ge, which means 'older brother.'

Anyway, when I came to the dining table for breakfast, Mama and Baba, our mother and father, were sitting in their chairs looking really nervous. Like they had big news they didn't want to tell us. I'd seen that look once before when Mama told us were getting our little brother, Ming Ming. But that was good news (at least, mostly. Sometimes Ming Ming could be a bit annoying). From the looks on their faces now, I could tell this would not be as good.

I turned to Ge Ge. "Uh oh. I have a feeling we're about to get into big trouble."

He nodded, a small smile on his face. "Yeah, get the gas masks ready. They're gonna explode."

I had to bite back a laugh since our parents were right in front of us. It would be so awkward if I laughed at Ge Ge's joke and Mama or Baba asked us what we were laughing at!

"Mama?" I asked, once I had regained my composure, "Is everything alright?" I suspected I knew what their news was. I heard them whispering about it for a long time.

Mama swallowed nervously *"Zao shang hao.* Good morning. Come children, sit. There is something that your baba and I have to tell you."

Two-year-old Ming Ming was sitting in his highchair, banging his spoon on the side of his soymilk bowl and yelling, "A MARY GWA! A MARY GWA!"

I looked at Ge Ge, alarmed, trying to send him a silent message with my eyes. He seemed to get it.

"America?" he whispered in Chinese.

I nodded and quickly turned back to Mama. "Yes, Mama?" I asked, also speaking Chinese.

Baba took over. "Luolan, Lizhong, we have made a decision. The Xia family is moving."

"To Liu's neighborhood?" Ge Ge asked half-heartedly.

Ge Ge's best friends from school, Liu Yong and Liu Qiang, were super rich and lived in a big, fancy neighborhood. I knew we probably weren't moving there, but it was a nice thought.

"No, dear," Mama said. "We're moving to *Mei Guo*. To America."

"What?" Ge Ge and I both yelled, even though we had pretty much guessed it already. "Why?"

I felt like Mama dropped a bomb on my head, though I already heard them talking about it. I didn't want to move to America. What was wrong with our life here?

"You children need a better education," Baba explained. "You'll like it there, trust me."

"But I like it here!" I blurted. "I like my friends, and my school, and everything!"

"We're moving," Baba said firmly. "And that is the end of the discussion. Now get a move on. You're going to be late for school! It's your last day!"

As I walked to Yuying School with my friend Haiqing Xu. I thought about the move, about school, about everything. Have you ever walked to school? Well, if you ever walked to school before, you know it's a great time for thinking. At least it is if your best friend isn't sneezing all over you.

"Haiqing, do you mind?" I asked her.

"*Dui bu qi!*" she murmured. "I breathed in some dust. But what happened to you? You're so quiet! Usually you're chattering away and I can barely get a word in!"

I hesitated to tell her. Haiqing was my best friend at Yuying, I knew that she would be heartbroken if I left.

"*Hao*," I relented. "I'll tell you, but you have to promise not to cry."

Haiqing looked at me questioningly. "Okay?"

"Well," I told her. "Just now, at breakfast, Mama told us that we are moving. To America."

Haiqing broke down crying. She was very sensitive. We were at Yuying now. I punched Haiqing in the shoulder.

"Shape up, we're at school now."

Haiqing sniffled. "I can't believe it, you're my best friend! I don't have any other friends as nice as you!"

I nodded. "I know, I don't have friends as awesome as you either. Now please be quiet, Haiqing."

As Haiqing and I filed into the building, an annoying boy named Dongqiang Zhang whispered, "Hey, Luolan! I hear we have a test today! Also, your hair looks like a *niao chao*!"

I stuck my tongue out at him for saying that my hair looked like a bird's nest but inside I groaned, feeling like I had a backpack stuffed with bricks. I don't mind the usual end-of-week test, but a surprise test on Monday? That was the worst thing ever. Especially on the last day of school!

"Alright, *tong xue men!*" my fifth grade math teacher Wang Lao Shi announced as she came into the classroom after our morning reading class. "Happy last day of school. Put your textbooks away, then come get your test papers!"

No one made a sound, but I could tell we were all groaning inside as we lined up to get our papers.

As Wang Lao Shi started the timer, I looked down on the test. It was so easy that it made me wonder if it was for fourth grade. Maybe

Wang Lao Shi meant for it to be a prank, or maybe ... *Stop!* I told myself. I was always doing this, thinking about how easy the test was instead of doing it. I started on the test, 11 times 10, *easy* 110...

Later, at the end of the day, as we were walking home from school, I picked up on my previous conversation with Haiqing. "Seriously, Haiqing, it's not so bad, I can visit you in the summer and text you."

Haiqing looked like she was about to cry again. "But what am I ever gonna do without you?"

"I'm taking this more calmly than you, Haiqing, and *I'm* the one who's moving."

She sighed. "Come over for a few minutes. We need to talk."

At Haiqing's house, we greeted Mrs. Xu politely and headed to Haiqing's room. We had a little while to talk before I had to go home to take care of Ming Ming while Mama ran errands.

"Haiqing," I said, looking at my friend in the eye, "you know I have to move." Despite how confident I tried to sound, I was truly terrified.

Haiqing sniffled and nodded. "But Luolan, I'll miss you so much!"

I hugged her. "Well, we aren't moving until next month," I replied, though deep down, my heart was breaking.

Now, I truly understood how bad it was going to be. I wouldn't be walking to school in the mornings with Haiqing. I wouldn't be complaining about how annoying Dongqiang Zhang was. I wouldn't be sharing secrets with my friend, and I wouldn't even be taking those annoying math tests! I would be in America, trying to learn proper English, and riding a *school bus*. I didn't want to leave China. Not one tiny bit.

* * *

It's the day, it's the day, I thought to myself as I finished packing my suitcases. Haiqing's mother was driving us to the airport since we had already sold our car. Haiqing was coming too, for final goodbyes.

"Luolan!" Ge Ge called to me. *"Kuai guo lai!* I need to ask you something!"

I put my last book from school into my book bag and entered his room. "Yes?" I asked him.

"Which one do you think I should take?" he asked me, holding up two card games.

"Seriously?" I asked, exasperated. "Mama said we shouldn't take too much stuff."

He shrugged. "I'm not leaving my cards behind."

"Well if that's the case," I told him, "then I guess you should take both."

I walked out of his room and back into mine. I looked around my room for the last time. This beautiful apartment, this had been my home for so long, and now we were moving across the world. Who knew if we'd ever come back?

"Luolan!" This time it was Haiqing. "Luolan! We're here!"

I ran to the door and opened it. There was Haiqing, a good friend to the end, holding a long box.

"Here," she said, wiping yet another tear away. "This is for you."

I opened the box. Inside, I found a long soft-tipped brush, an inkwell, and an ink stick. A piece of rice paper read Xia Luo Lan in Chinese characters. My name.

"Oh, Haiqing!" I hugged her. You're the best *peng you* ever!"

As we got into the car, Mama asked, "Lizhong, did you remember your toothbrush?"

"Mama!"

"Alright, alright, let's get going."

The drive that came next was one of the worst, longest, most boring things I had ever been forced to endure. It was sad, because both Haiqing and I knew that soon we would be apart. I would be flying to America and Haiqing, well, she would be stuck back in China.

Haiqing must have sensed my thoughts because she tried to comfort me. "Don't worry so much, Luolan. We'll be together again someday. Besides, it's just like you said. We can text and Skype each other."

I wasn't cheered up much, especially since Haiqing sounded so unsure, but I managed a weak smile.

"We're here!" Haiqing's mother called.

"*Zai jian*, Haiqing," I whispered. "I'll miss you."

Haiqing nodded. "Goodbye, Luolan. Remember, we'll be together again someday."

She wasn't certain. I could tell that just by looking into her face, but there was really no point arguing with her since we were about to be separated.

I just nodded.

Mrs. Xu stopped her car and we climbed out. Haiqing did too. She waved as we shuffled into the airport. Even as we turned the corner and out of sight, I could still see her half-sad, half-smiling face in my mind, scrunched up to hold back her tears, and her hand waving back and forth in a final goodbye.

We got to the front desk to check our baggage. We'd filled up nine suitcases and four bags. One of the suitcases was too heavy and the airline wouldn't allow it, so we had to leave some things behind. The airport would ship them back to our old house. I hoped the new people who moved into our apartment would find the things useful.

We couldn't check my cello (yes, I play cello) along with the other baggage, so we had to buy a ticket for it, too. At least it didn't take up as much room as Ge Ge!

Ge Ge stated flatly that he'd forgotten his toothbrush. He should've listened to Mama. Ming Ming cried that he didn't have his rubber duck. I remembered that I forgot my favorite pleasure reading book in my desk.

After we checked our baggage and got our boarding passes, we stepped into the line for the Immigration Inspection. The line was so long, especially with Ge Ge complaining about his toothbrush and my cello weighing me down.

After we finally got out, we went through the metal detector. Then we sat down to wait. I took out my second favorite book and started to read. Pretty soon I got bored of it. I asked Mama if I could take a look in the nearby stores. She said yes.

I went into one of the toy stores making sure I stayed where Mama and Baba could see me. There were stuffed pandas and bamboo displayed on the shelves. My heart ached again when I thought about leaving China. America seemed so large and empty. I wished we didn't have to go.

"Flight number 23," a voice on the loudspeaker announced, cutting through my thoughts.

I hurried back to my family. They stood and slipped into line for boarding check. The girl in front of us looked nice. She had long curly brown hair and tan skin.

My first American. She turned and saw me.

"Oh, hi!" she greeted me. "My name is Olivia, Olivia Deacon. What's yours?"

I waved. "Xia Luolan."

She looked confused. "So is your name Xia or Luo or Lan?"

"All."

"Huh?"

"No mind."

"I don't have a mind?"

Why hadn't I bothered to pay attention in English class at school? I hated myself.

"You have mind. Sorry if I insult."

Olivia looked dazed. I felt bad for confusing her. My first American girl and I had already made a bad impression.

"Luolan!" Mama called over to me. "We're boarding, come on!"

The plane was a lot cleaner than I'd expected. I didn't know what to expect since I had never been on a plane in my life (yes I'd never been out of the country before), so I just pictured it as around the same quality as the subway we rode on last month.

"Hey Luolan, please don't mess everything up and embarrass me on our first airplane ride." I did my best to glare at him. "*You* mess everything up, Ge Ge, so be quiet."

Our seats were nice since they were in Business Class. Ming Ming sat with Mama and Baba while Ge Ge, my cello, and I sat behind them.

"Get the throw-up bag," Mama warned. "The take-offs can be shaky."

"C'mon, Mama," Ge Ge rolled his eyes. "They can't be worse than the rides at Wilderness Adventure."

Wilderness Adventure was an amusement park we went to last summer. Ge Ge, being tall enough for most of the rides, rode on a really scary roller coaster. When he came down, he was all shaky and threw up two times before he felt well enough to walk.

"Still," Mama told him. "Get the throw-up bag ready."

I thought we should listen to her. She was correct about Ge Ge forgetting his toothbrush, after all. But when I reached for the throw-up bag, Ge Ge laughed at me, so I put it back.

"Remember, kids," Baba said to us. "This is a once-in-a-lifetime experience. Treasure it. Come on! We're moving! To the Land of Opportunity!"

Ge Ge and I laughed, but Baba's words stuck in my mind. Was this really that wonderful of an experience? I honestly didn't want to move out of China, so why should I treasure the memory?

Soon the pilot turned on the seatbelt sign. Ge Ge and I buckled up and I pulled my strap tight. No use taking any chances. Ge Ge saw what I was doing and rolled his eyes again. This time I rolled mine back at him.

Then the plane began to move. I laid my head back on the headrest and closed my eyes. I was surprised when I felt Ge Ge's hand slip into mine. It was shaking.

"I thought you weren't scared," I said.

He grinned. "I'm an awesome liar, remember?"

I glanced around the cabin. Olivia Deacon, the American girl, was sitting in the seat across from mine. She waved. I waved back.

"Don't worry," she whispered. "It hardly ever kills people."

My eyes widened, but then I remembered that Americans didn't usually mean what they say.

"You ... not telling truth, right?" I asked her in my broken English.

"Yeah, I'm not." Olivia leaned across the aisle and squeezed my other hand. "Don't worry, it's perfectly safe. I've been on many planes and they never crash-land or anything. Just a little turbulence." I had no idea what turbulence was and Olivia must've read my expression because she added, "Turbulence means bumpy air."

I nodded and turned to my TV screen. The TV was playing a safety video. It turned out there was a life jacket (whatever that was) under the seat, and air masks (what was that?) would drop from the compartment on top if the air pressure got too low.

When the safety video ended, the plane began gliding down the runway. Olivia had been right. The takeoff wasn't too bad. Before I knew it, we were in the air. I sighed.

"Goodbye, China." I whispered. Then I turned back to my TV screen. Our trip had begun.

Oh Wow . . . America

"I am so tired!" Ge Ge complained.

Mama yawned, too.

"The time is different here," she explained. "It's three thirty in the morning back in China. Our bodies aren't used to being up so early, so we're all tired."

I noticed she hadn't said "home". I understood why. America was supposed to be our home now. Although it didn't really feel like home at the moment.

"We need to get to Immigration Inspection," Baba told us. No one really cared, we were all too tired.

After the inspection, we got all our luggage. Bad luck for me, I had to carry the two heaviest bags *and* my cello -which I practiced every night- on my back. My arms were practically falling off by the time we got to the taxi.

"Hey," the driver said. "I'm Mike."

"Hi." Ge Ge was better at English than I was, so he took over. "I'm Lizhong, this is my sister Luolan. Can you get us to the Hyatt hotel, please? We have nine suitcases, four bags."

"Okay, Li Own," the driver replied, mispronouncing Ge Ge's name. He began hoisting our suitcases into the trunk of his car.

Mama, Ge Ge, and I climbed into the back of the car, Mama holding Ming Ming. Baba sat in front to give directions.

I pulled out my book from my bag and began to read, but the Chinese words seemed unfamiliar. I closed the book. Apparently, in America they only allowed English letters to look familiar, not Chinese characters.

As we drove, I looked out at the street signs. I could recognize some of the words on them like STOP, and NO TURN ON RED. But the other ones looked jumbled and unfamiliar.

"Mama?" I asked. "Is there WiFi here? I want to email Haiqing."

Mama shook her head. "We have to link onto the WiFi in America," she explained. "Wait until we get to the hotel."

I sat still for the rest of the ride. Ge Ge gazed out the window. Ming Ming scrunched up in Mama's lap. Finally, Mike stopped the taxi.

"We're here," he announced. He opened the door for Ge Ge and me, then he went to the trunk to help Baba with the luggage.

This time I lugged the 'baby care and toys' suitcase. It was considerably lighter than the other suitcases I previously carried. It contained all of Ming Ming's things and a few of my heavier books, toys, and stuffed animals. It also contained Ge Ge's English flashcards. I also took my backpack and the 'other items' bag.

Once we entered the hotel lobby, Baba walked to the front desk to check in. I sat down on a sofa with Ge Ge and took out my phone. I connected it to the Wifi and typed a message to Haiqing. I waited a long time for an answer before I remembered the time difference.

Ge Ge stretched out on the couch and yawned. "I think I'm gonna take a nap."

I poked him in the ribs. "We're in public, Ge Ge, stop it."

He groaned. "I'm tired."

"So am I." I showed him my phone screen. "Look at this new app I downloaded last week. It's called Pigs Ahoy. It's an American game."

Ge Ge and I played Pigs Ahoy until Baba called to us. We followed him into the elevator and Baba pressed the 13 button.

"We're number 2024," he told us.

The elevator dinged to a stop. Our family stepped out. I breathed in the fresh air. Just then I noticed a girl with curly brown hair walking toward the elevator.

"Hey, it's Olivia!" I cried to my family. Then to Olivia. "Hi Olivia!"

Olivia turned and her face brightened. "Hey, mom!" she called to her mother. "It's Luolan! The girl from the plane!" So she did know my name after all.

"Oh, hi!" Mrs. Deacon said. "It's nice to meet you, Luolan, Olivia told us about you."

"We're meeting friends at the hotel," Olivia explained. "We're not staying, but I'll give you my number and we can text or something."

"Where you live?" I asked.

"29 Woodbury Lane." Olivia told me. "That's in Winston."

"We will live on Woodbury Lane too!" I exclaimed. Mama had been talking about where we were going to live on the airplane. "28, I think."

"Right next door!" Olivia grinned. "What school are you gonna be in?"

"Andrew Jackson Middle School, I think," I replied.

"Me too!" Olivia laughed. "So we won't have to say goodbye, after all!"

Baba cleared his throat. "Luolan," he interrupted quietly. "We have to get to our room."

I translated what Baba said to Olivia and she pouted. "I'll come with you!" she pleaded eagerly. "Can I?"

"Please, Baba?" I begged. "We won't be any trouble and she can return to her family afterwards!"

Mama nodded. "Yes. It will be a good bonding experience for you girls."

"We'll meet you downstairs in the lounge at five, Olivia," Olivia's father told her. "Is that OK with you?" he asked Baba.

Baba smiled. "It will be okay," he replied to Mr. Deacon. Then we all trooped into the room.

We burst through the room eagerly. It was pretty large, larger than other hotels I'd been in. There was a sofa, which, according to Mama, turned into a bed and two smaller beds, all with white sheets. There was a bathroom and a desk and closet. There was also a minibar.

"Wow!" Olivia breathed. "You got one of the suites!" Seeing my puzzled look, she added, "A suite is a big room in a hotel." Then she offered me an orange stick. "Want some gum?"

I hesitated, but she coaxed me and finally I took it and popped the stick in my mouth. It tasted of oranges and mangoes and pineapples.

"Yum!"

"It's called Tropical Island," Olivia told me.

"In China, only has boring names," I joked. "Like Pear and Banana and Mixed Berry."

We broke down laughing. Then, Olivia said, "Hey, Luolan, can we exchange emails?"

"Yes!" I cried. "I did not think of that!"

Olivia wrote her email on a piece of paper. I wrote mine on another.

"Now we can communicate," Olivia said happily. Then she added, "that means--"

"Talk." I smiled. "Yes, I know."

Soon, it was time for Olivia to leave. I hugged her goodbye. "See you soon," I said.

"Very soon," Olivia grinned. "We're going on a cruise soon. Maybe you can come with us."

"When?" I questioned.

"Beginning of August," Olivia replied.

"Can I invite friend from China, Haiqing?" I asked her.

"Sure!" Olivia hugged me. "We can talk more later. But I have to go now or else Mom and Dad will be mad."

She headed out the door and shut it behind her. That was when I noticed it was almost 6:10. Haiqing was normally up early during summer vacation. I typed a message to her and her reply came almost instantly.

Luolan: Haiqing, I met this girl named Olivia Deacon at the airport. She's really nice and she invited us to go on a cruise with her!

Haiqing:	Seriously? Your first American! What does she look like?
Luolan:	Brown hair, tan skin.
Haiqing:	Cool! Are you tired yet?
Luolan:	Really. But you should see Ge Ge. He's snoring like my baba!
Haiqing:	Uh oh. My baba's calling me. Better go.
Luolan:	Bye.

I closed the app and played Pigs Ahoy until I felt unbearably tired. Then I took my toothbrush out of the suitcase, brushed my teeth, changed, and climbed onto the sofa bed.

"Ge Ge?" I whispered.

"Mm-hm?" he murmured, half-asleep.

"You think you're gonna fit in here?"

"Dunno," he shrugged. "I suppose we're just gonna have to do the best we can do, aren't we?"

"I guess," I sighed. "I don't--" I turned and saw that Ge Ge had already fallen asleep.

I settled in and tried to fall asleep, but I couldn't despite how tired I was. I picked up my notepad and pencil and made a list.

Things I Want to Accomplish in America: 1. Make three new friends. 2. Learn English. 3. Get people to like me. 4. Find a reason to call America 'home'.

* * *

"Come on!" Ge Ge called, skipping ahead of me and up the driveway of our new house. "Don't you wanna come see?"

"Of course I want to see!" I replied. "It's the house I'll be living in for the rest of my life! If you'd just wait..."

Ge Ge just laughed and danced ahead.

I shook my head. *Brothers.* I opened the door.

"It's so *mei li!*" I breathed as I stepped into our new house. "It's so shiny and empty and clean!"

"It won't be empty for long," Mama announced. "We're all going out to buy furniture this week. Do you kids want to see your rooms?"

"Yes, please!" we both said eagerly.

We raced up the stairs. Our rooms were next to each other, but far apart enough to give us each some privacy. My room was painted pale blue and had two windows. A light shaped like a flower hung from the ceiling. A wardrobe that was connected to the wall stood to the left of where the bed used to be. A painting of a sailboat hung on the opposite wall to the wardrobe.

"It's wonderful," I breathed. Then I raced over to see Ge Ge's room.

His walls were painted to resemble a zoo. My guess was that a little boy had been living there before. When I started to laugh, Ge Ge rolled his eyes at me.

"If you see any gray wallpaper, let me know," he muttered. "What I'm ever gonna do if I'm caught with this thing on my walls, I don't know."

"Children, I'm going shopping for groceries," Mama called up. "Anyone want to come?"

"I'll go," I told her. "I want to see an American grocery store."

Ge Ge said he wanted to stay home and plan his room decoration. Baba needed to send some emails to his partners at work. So we went alone.

Mama got into the car Baba had rented online a few days ago. She was going to get an American driver's license next week, but for now she could use her Chinese one. I sat in the backseat, wanting to explore every inch of our new car.

As we drove, I asked Mama, "Do you think I'll fit in at school?"

Mama glanced at me. "I do," she replied. "I'm sure of it."

"Are you absolutely sure?"

"Yes." Mama smiled at me. "Do you remember that time when my boss promoted me to a higher position at work?"

I nodded. Everyone knew about that promotion.

"Well," Mama went on, "when I went to the meeting, I wasn't sure that I'd fit in with the higher, more experienced officers. But we got along fine, and I even made some new friends." She laughed gently. "Of course you'll fit in, my *hai zi*. You will."

We pulled into the parking lot at the supermarket. Two words were printed on the roof of the store. WHOLE FOODS.

"What does whole mean?" Mama asked.

"Um, it's like wholesome," I tried to explain. She still looked confused. "Real, maybe, full."

"Ah." Mama took my hand. "Let's go inside."

Inside, it was sort of like a Chinese grocery store, but emptier. There was an aisle for pastries, an aisle for fruit, an aisle for frozen goods, and an aisle for vegetables. There was also an aisle for clothes and other things.

"What do we need to get?" I asked Mama.

She laughed. "Everything! How about you get the veggies and fruit while I go get the household things?"

"Sure." I pushed my cart towards the veggie aisle. There were mushrooms, carrots, bananas, and apples. I picked up a few of each, except for the things that looked weird. I made sure to pick up lots of peaches, since peaches symbolize long life in China.

Then I went to find Mama. She was standing in the vitamin aisle looking confused.

"Which one do I get?" she asked me. "There are so many different types of vitamins!"

I read the labels. "I think the solid ones are for adults and the soft ones are for kids, Mama," I told her, picking up one of each.

"Thanks," she replied. "I'll be careful to learn more English so we can go shopping easily."

Then we moved onto the yogurt aisle. There were so many types of yogurt! I picked the ones that had chocolate chips and pretzels mixed in. Mama took the strawberry. As we were moving to the check-out counter, I noticed an ice cream stand next to the pastry aisle.

"Mama!" I said. "Can I get some ice cream?"

She started to protest but I did my best puppy-dog eyes at her and she relented. "Okay, but a small one."

I grinned. No one could resist my puppy-dog eyes. I got a green tea cone and we walked to the check-out counter.

"Good day, ladies," the cashier said to us. He looked about college-age, just a few years older than Ge Ge.

"Hi," I said to him. "We check-out."

He grinned. "That's what you came here for."

We put all our items on the table and the cashier pretended to faint. "Woah, did you just move here or something?"

I nodded. "Got here today."

The cashier scanned the items one by one, then he motioned for Mama to swipe her card. Mama pulled out her American credit card and swiped it. Then she signed her name in Chinese. Next, he put our groceries in bags and handed them to us. There were five bags total.

I licked my cone as we got into the car. Having explored the back thoroughly, I started to get into the front seat before Mama stopped me.

"Here, you have to be thirteen to sit in the front," she explained.

"Seriously?" I asked.

"Yes," Mama replied. "Now get into the back. We need to unpack and then go out for dinner. We haven't unpacked our pots and pans so we can't cook."

"Oh." I climbed into the back and fastened my seatbelt. So many rules in America. Would I really like it here?

A New Experience

"I'll take the blue bed," I said in Mandarin, pointing to the blue bed with the lavender comforter.

"And I'll take the gray wallpaper and the black bed," Ge Ge added.

"I'll have the pale blue desk and the white fuzzy chair."

"I'll take the black desk and the black chair."

"Can I have the white bookshelf?"

"Can I have that white chair?"

"Can I have the gray nightstand?"

"Can I have the ninja star collection?"

"Can I have the blue box?"

"Can I--"

"STOP!" Mama held up her hands. "Yes, yes, yes, no, yes."

"Hurray!" I cheered, while Ge Ge sulked.

"Why did you say yes to all of Luolan's and no to one of mine?" he complained, also speaking Chinese.

"Because you don't need ninja stars," Mama explained patiently. "You can have everything else."

"Fine," Ge Ge sighed. "But the ninja stars are really cool."

"You'll get some Pokémon cards," Mama told him. She knew Ge Ge loved cards.

"What are those?" Ge Ge asked, obviously interested.

"Kids are obsessed with them in America," Mama replied. "We'll buy you some later."

"What do I get?" I asked.

"We'll get you a library account," Mama said to me. "And a library card. You can check out your own books."

That sounded awesome to me. At my school back in China we didn't have a library, so I had to buy all my books. But from what I'd heard, there was a public library just a few blocks away.

We browsed some more. Finally, we got to the checkout counter. "Can ship furniture to home?" Mama asked the cashier.

"Sure," the cashier replied. "Where do you live?"

"28, Woodbury Lane, Winston," Mama told him,

"Cool." The cashier smiled. "Can I get your phone number?"

Mama told him her phone number and email.

"OK, so when do you want it shipped?" he asked.

"As soon as possible." Mama said.

"So, in a week?" he asked.

"Is that good deal?" Mama asked before Ge Ge and I could stop her. Mama hadn't meant to offend the cashier, but she just hadn't known how to say 'is that the shortest amount of time?' Now it sounded like she was being skeptical of the store's quality,

"Yes," the cashier replied firmly. "Now, there are other shoppers..."

Ge Ge and I herded Mama out the door. She looked confused. "What did I do?"

"You weren't supposed to say 'is that a good deal', Mama," Ge Ge told her. "That offended the cashier."

"Ah." Mama winced. "Sorry, kids."

"Yeah, it's fine." Just then my phone rang. I took it out of my pocket and pressed the TALK button.

"Hello?"

"Luolan!" It was Olivia. "Bad news, the cruise got cancelled because it didn't have enough money or something, but good news, we're going camping!"

"What is camping?" I asked her.

"Oh, it's great fun," she replied. "You sleep under the stars and roast marshmallows. Your family can come, too! But you'll have to bring your own tent. You can invite Haiqing, too."

"When?" I asked. "And where?"

"Beginning of August." she said. "And it's at this camping place just north from here, in the mountains. They have a lot of trees there."

"Oh."

"You OK?"

"Yes, but why you do not come and play? Your house is close."

Olivia laughed. "Hey, why didn't I think of that? I'll be right over." And she hung up.

"*Mama*!" I screamed. "*Olivia's coming*!"

"Ouch!" Ge Ge whined. "No need to screech. You have a real loud voice, Luolan."

I punched him in the arm. "So did you when you were a baby. Mama told me."

"Wasn't she just over yesterday?" Mama asked.

"Yes, but she's coming again." I said. "Hurry! We need to be there before her so we can welcome her!"

We all climbed into the car and Mama exceeded the speed limit a few times. When we finally pulled into the driveway, Olivia's car was already parked in front of our house.

"*She's here*!" I squealed.

Ge Ge covered his ears. "Agh! I think I'm going deaf."

I ran up the stairs and through the front path. I burst through the door where Olivia was greeting Baba.

"Oops," I muttered, embarrassed. "Sorry."

Olivia laughed and hugged me. "I just told your father about the camping trip!" she exclaimed. "And guess what? He said *yes*!"

I pulled away from Olivia and hugged Baba. "*Xie xie*, Baba! Thank you thank you thank you!" I squealed, just as Ge Ge came over.

He groaned. "I'm going to my room."

"There's nothing in your room," I reminded him. "At least, nothing except monkey zoo wallpaper."

"Good point." He sighed and retreated into the empty dining room.

"Luolan, do you want to pick our classes for this semester together?" Olivia asked me. "I brought my iPad."

"Sure! Let me ask Mom to send me the link."

A few minutes later, we were sprawled out on the floor picking out classes for the quarter.

"It says we have to take math, science, history, health, gym, a language of choice, an art elective and English," I told Olivia.

"I'm taking Chinese," Olivia said. "You should, too. It's super fun and we get to play games all the time."

"Okay," I replied. "I already speak Chinese anyway."

"Which art elective are you taking?" Olivia asked.

"Theater, maybe," I told her. "What about you?"

"Me too."

Olivia high-fived me. When we were finally done with our selections, we sprawled on the floor wondering what to do next. I groaned inwardly, thinking of all the unpacking I would have to help with once Olivia was gone. Wait … unpacking …

"Hey, can you help unpack?" I asked Olivia. "I mean, my room. Not whole house."

Sure!" Olivia replied happily. "I can't wait to see what you brought."

We lugged my two suitcases up the stairs and into my room. "OK," Olivia said, taking charge. "First, clothes."

"I like sorted pants and shirts," I told her. "And separate for dresses and other things."

Olivia nodded. "Got it."

We began sorting the clothes into piles. Pile Warm Color, Pile Cool Color, Pile Other Colors, Pile Dresses, Pile Undergarments, Pile Socks, Pile Jackets, Pile Winter Things, and Pile All the Other Stuff.

When we finally placed all the folded piles in the closet, we shut the door and sat down, exhausted.

"Wow, this is tiring," Olivia announced, breathing heavily. Then she noticed something silver at the top of the suitcase. "You have a laptop computer?"

I blushed. "Present for birthday."

"Cool!" Olivia exclaimed. "What do you do on it?"

"Write fiction," I told her. "Articles for news, too."

"You write for the newspaper?" Olivia asked, wide-eyed.

I laughed. "No, friend newspaper. Haiqing, me, and few other girls from old class. English teacher, too."

"Cool. Well, we should get back to work. Shall we unpack the bathroom?"

"I have my own," I replied. "Here." I showed her the small bathroom that was connected to my room.

"Lucky," Olivia said. "What did you bring?"

"Toothbrush," I told her. "Towels, comb, cups. Also slippers. And a few other things."

"Nice." Olivia smiled brightly. "Shall we?"

* * *

'Haiqing,' I typed at six o'clock that night. 'Are you there?'

'Hi Luolan!' Haiqing typed back. 'I met this new girl named Ziwei yesterday. She's super nice and you'd really like her'.

I felt a pang of jealousy when I read those words. Haiqing had found a new best friend? Then I thought about what Haiqing must've felt when I told her about Olivia Deacon. I decided to support her friendship with Ziwei.

'Great!' I typed. 'I'm happy for you.'

No answer. She was probably heading out to play with Ziwei. Just then, my stomach grumbled. Because of my visit with Olivia, I missed lunch. Ge Ge poked his head into my room.

"Hungry?" he asked. I nodded. "We brought you some food from McDonalds."

I raced down the stairs with my empty stomach leading me. There was a McDonalds box on the counter. Inside the box were some fries, a carton of milk, and a fish sandwich.

As I was eating my sandwich, Ge Ge ran down the stairs, chased by Ming Ming.

"Help!" he mock-screamed. "The crocodile's gonna eat meeeeeee!"

I groaned. "Talk about being loud, Ge Ge." Then to Ming Ming, "Why don't you get your crayons out, Ming Ming?" I asked. "You can draw a picture of a crocodile."

Ming Ming scrambled up the stairs to get his crayons, leaving Ge Ge and me in the kitchen.

"You're good with kids, you know," Ge Ge told me. "Maybe you would consider a babysitting job."

"Me?" I laughed, thinking he was joking. "I wouldn't be any good at it."

"Oh, maybe." Ge Ge hesitated. "I met a girl."

I wiggled my eyebrows. "And?"

"While you were buying groceries, a girl stopped by on the way to the library. She has a little brother and her mom and dad are really busy, so her brother needs a babysitter while she's gone."

"And you're asking me?" I asked, surprised.

"Please, Luolan?" Ge Ge pleaded. "I'll pay you."

"How much?"

"Fifty renminbi."

"Seventy."

"Fine." Ge Ge grinned at me. "Will you do it?"

"Maybe. Do you have a crush on her?"

Ge Ge made a face. "And what if I do?"

"Aww. Okay. When is the job?"

"Tomorrow."

"*Tomorrow*?" I shrieked.

Ge Ge covered his ears and nodded. "Yeah, plenty of time to prepare. By the way, the kid's name is William Baker. The girl is Clara. Bye!" He ducked out the door before I could start yelling at him.

I sighed. Tomorrow. Plenty of time, sure. For eating a fish sandwich. I finished my sandwich and fries and drank my milk. Then I took out my laptop computer and did a search: how to be a good babysitter.

* * *

"Hi Mrs. Baker," I greeted William's mom the next day. "Hi William."

"I'm Will," William said.

"Of course."

"Hi Luolan." A girl about Ge Ge's age came out from behind Mrs. Baker. "I'm Clara. Lizhong's told me all about you."

"He did?" I asked, wondering what Ge Ge said about me.

"Don't worry." Clara laughed. "Only good things."

"Come in, Luolan," Mrs. Baker welcomed me. I stepped into the Bakers' house.

"Here are the emergency numbers," Mrs. Baker said, pointing to a paper tacked up on a bulletin board. "I'll be at the grocery store and Clara'll be next door. My husband's phone is getting fixed so you won't be able to contact him, but if anything goes wrong, Clara's and my phone numbers are on there. Will is in kindergarten. He likes coloring and playing UNO. Don't let him eat too many snacks or watch too much TV. OK?"

I nodded. I had problems speaking English, but I could understand it just fine. "OK," I agreed.

"Good." Mrs. Baker tugged on her shoes and grabbed her car keys. "Bye!"

When she was out the door, I turned to Clara. "I have a question."

"Yeah?"

"Are you going to ask again for me as babysitter?"

Clara shrugged. "It depends on if Will likes you. If he likes you OK, then we'll hire you permanently."

I nodded. "OK."

"I'd better get going now," Clara said to me. "Good luck."

"Thanks." Then Clara stepped out the door and Will and I were alone.

"So," I said to Will. "What do you want to do?"

Will shrugged. "Dunno. Babysitters are boring."

"What do you mean?" I asked him.

"They always just sit down on the couch and check their phones all day," Will explained. "If it's not emails, they text their boyfriends. Are you going to text your boyfriend?"

I laughed. "I'm only eleven. I don't have a boyfriend."

"Are ya gonna check your email?" Will asked.

"Don't have phone," I replied.

"Good."

Just then I had an idea. "Will, you like to draw?"

"Yup."

"Do you have ink?"

"Yup."

"Do you have brush?"

"Yup."

I grinned. "You can get them for me? We will be busy today. I have a surprise for you, Will."

Surprises, Tents, and Other Stuff

We finished writing the characters just in time for Mrs. Baker and Clara to come home. Clara was first. Her hair was messed up and she looked happy.

"So," she said brightly. "What did you guys do?"

"We have a surprise!" Will squealed.

"A surprise?" A man's voice asked. It was Mr. Baker. "Well!"

I brought out the banner we'd made. "We made while you were gone." I told the Bakers. "It's Chinese calligraphy. *Shu fa*. The banner says, 'My name is Will Baker'."

Mrs. Baker looked at the banner. "Wow!" she exclaimed. "These characters are so pretty!"

Mr. Baker and Clara both nodded and smiled.

"You're good with kids." Mrs. Baker said, smiling. "We're gonna recommend you to our friends."

"Recommend?" I asked.

"That means tell them about you," Mr. Baker explained. "And tell them that they should hire you."

"Me?" I asked. "They should hire ME?"

"Yeah, you." Mr. Baker laughed and handed me a bill. "Here, take this."

"I'm paid?" I asked him in amazement.

"Of course!" Mr. Baker smiled. "You took care of Will."

"I never told I'm paid."

"Well, you are," Clara said with mock sternness, slapping the bill into my hand. "So take it and stop complaining."

Everyone laughed, then Mr. Baker announced, "You'd better be getting back to your house now, Luolan. Want me to drive you?"

I shook my head. "House very close," I told him. "I walk."

"Bye, Luolan!" Will called after me as I exited the house.

When I got to my house, I took out my phone and called Olivia. She answered right away, screaming in my ear.

"*The camping trip is in two weeeeks!!!*"

I covered my ear. "Olivia, I'm lucky if I not go deaf!" I complained.

Olivia laughed. "Sorry. I'm just really excited."

"Yeah, me too," I agreed. "Haiqing is coming next week for eight days!"

"Yeah, about that," Olivia said, suddenly serious. "I don't think we don't have enough tents for three kids.

"That's OK," I reassured her. "Haiqing and I can share tent."

"Yeah, but--" Just then, Olivia's mom said something and Olivia sighed. "Gotta go. Dentist appointment."

"Bye." I hung up and slipped my phone back into my pocket. What had Olivia meant when she was talking about Haiqing and the tent?

Was it possible she was jealous of my friendship with Haiqing? No. It couldn't be. And yet, it was the most likely prospect.

I shook my head. I just had to stop worrying and start counting down the days to the camping trip.

The furniture came a week later, like promised. So did Haiqing. I exchanged my renminbi from Ge Ge for American dollars and bought a book with the money. It was called *Judy Moody* and it didn't look very hard, nor very easy.

With the leftover money I bought a box of American cookies called Oreos. On the outside they were chocolate cookie and on the inside a kind of frosting. They were delicious.

When Haiqing came to our house, we both screamed and hugged each other, jumping up and down at the same time.

"You're here!" I screamed. "You're here, you're here, you're here!"

"I can't believe I'm seeing you again, Luolan!" Haiqing screamed. Then quieter, "How's America?"

"Fun!" I replied. "I met a girl named Olivia, babysitted a boy named Will Baker, and ate Oreos! How is it back home?"

"Boring without you," Haiqing told me. "But I met this girl named Ziwei who's new to the neighborhood and she's pretty nice. Also, Dongqiang Zhang from our school is being SO annoying."

I giggled. "He never stops, does he?"

Haiqing shook her head. "No. But I can't believe we get to see each other after only a couple of weeks!"

"I know!" I grinned. "And I can't believe that you're going camping with Olivia and me!"

Haiqing's face creased into a frown. "Wait a moment. I thought it was only going to be you and me. I didn't know Olivia was coming."

I shook my head. "She's coming."

Just then, Olivia threw open the door. "I can't believe it's todaaay!" she sang. "The camping trip is-" She saw Haiqing. "Oh. Hi. I'm Olivia."

"I'm Haiqing," Haiqing replied. "Luolan tells me a lot about you."

Haiqing was a lot better at English than I was. Both Olivia and Haiqing looked kind of uncomfortable, so I talked to break the silence.

"Um, Haiqing," I asked her. "Did you bring your stuff?"

Haiqing snapped out of her stupor. "Um, yeah," she said. "I brought my sleeping bag and my clothes."

"Great!" I replied with forced cheerfulness. Then to Olivia, "When do we leave?"

The drive to the camping grounds was much like the drive to the airport in China, but much worse. It was weird how I'd been looking forward to Haiqing's visit so much, but now that she was here, we weren't chattering away like crows, like we usually did when we were together. I could sense the air stirring between Haiqing and Olivia. Yep, they were definitely jealous of each other.

Olivia's dad drove one car and Baba drove the other. Mama was staying home with Ming Ming. Haiqing, Olivia, and I were all crammed into the backseat of Olivia's dad's car.

"So!" Mr. Deacon cried with fake cheerfulness. "Are you girls psyched for the camping trip?"

Haiqing frowned. "What is 'psyched'?" she asked.

"It means 'excited'," Olivia tried to explain. "Or 'happy'."

That was pretty much the only conversation we had on the way there.

When we finally got to the campsite, Mr. Deacon signed us in at the Guest Registration Center and we got to pick our site. We chose a nice, serene spot beside the lake. I liked it, but with all the tension between Haiqing and Olivia, I couldn't properly appreciate it.

"Hey, Haiqing," I said to her that night as she was rolling out her sleeping bag. She turned toward me.

"Yeah, Luolan?"

"What's going on between you and Olivia?"

It seemed like the right question to ask. Then again, I definitely wasn't an Olympic gold medalist when it came to figuring out emotions.

Haiqing shook her head. "It's fine, Luolan. It's just . . . nothing. Never mind."

"What?"

She made a face. "Luolan, when someone tells you 'nothing,' it means 'nothing'."

My face burned bright red. "Haiqing, you know you can tell me anything, right?"

Haiqing nodded. "I do, Luolan, and I am grateful. But some things just . . . aren't meant to be shared."

I stopped myself from asking, 'Like what?' That would have been nosier.

Days passed and Haiqing grew more distant. The only times she talked to me were before lights out to tell me things about Ziwei.

"She's super nice," Haiqing would say. "We went to the mall together after school."

Those stories made me clench my fists and grit my teeth. Was Haiqing doing it on purpose? How could my best friend just start talking about her new friend while she could be having fun with me, her *old* friend?

So, during the daytime I hung out with Olivia. She taught me new American words and showed me hand games the girls in her class liked to play. Sometimes we brought Ge Ge along and he would show us how to climb trees, which he learned on a field trip. I got pretty good at it, considering I had grown up in the city.

At night we sat by the fire and roasted marshmallows. Mrs. Deacon taught us how to make s'mores and we had contests to see who could eat the most. Mr. Deacon and Baba always tied. It was fun to see them try and break the tie.

One morning, Olivia shook me out of my sleeping bag. It was Wednesday. We had come on Sunday, and we had five days left before we had to go back.

"Come on," she whispered. "Don't wake Haiqing. I have someone for you to meet."

I followed her out of the tent that Haiqing and I shared and into the woods. We emerged onto another clearing where two green tents sat side by side with a gray car in the middle.

"Um, sure this is a good idea?" I asked nervously.

Olivia laughed. "Relax," she said. "The people who live here are my friends. They're daughter, Ivie, is in my grade at school."

"Wait. *Live* here?"

Before Olivia could respond, a head emerged from the flap of the tent. When she saw us, her face broke into a grin.

"Olivia?" she asked. "Is that you?"

Olivia laughed. "Put on your glasses, Ivie."

Ivie's head disappeared into the tent. A moment later, she reappeared, this time wearing a pair of blue glasses that matched her sky blue eyes.

"Olivia!" she cried, her long red hair falling into her face as she hugged Olivia. "And you brought a friend!"

I decided that I liked her immediately.

"Ivie, this is Luolan Xia," Olivia introduced us. "Luolan, this is Ivalyn Anderbell. Ivie for short."

"Hey," we greeted each other.

"Olivia told me that she met a girl at the airport," Ivie told me. "By mail, of course. But she didn't say who."

"By mail?" I asked. "Don't you have a phone?"

Ivie winced, and Olivia elbowed me. "It's a sensitive subject," she whispered. "Don't ask!"

Ivie shook her head. "No, it's okay," she replied softly. Then she turned to me. "My family lives here at the campsite. We live in those tents over there."

"Really?" I asked before I could stop myself. "You *live at campsite?*" Then I winced. "Sorry if sounds nosy. Don't have to answer."

Ivie smiled sadly. "It's not your fault. A lot of people ask those questions. So don't worry."

"Ivie's gonna be in our grade in September," Olivia broke in. "I thought you guys might like to get to know each other beforehand."

We were all silent for a moment. Then a voice called from inside the tent.

"Hey Ivie," the voice said. "Who's out there?"

"It's just Olivia and Luolan, Austin," Ivie replied.

A boy about my age, maybe a year older, poked his head out of the tent. I glanced at Olivia, wondering who he was and saw that she was *blushing. Olivia. Blushing.* She caught my glance and quickly turned away, probably blushing even harder.

"Hi Austin," Olivia squeaked, once she got her face under control.

"Olivia!" Austin grinned. "Hey! Didn't expect to see you here!"

Ivie rolled her eyes at me. She made a disgusted face and we both desperately tried not to giggle.

"Nonsense!" Olivia replied coyly. "We're here every summer!"

"Anyway," Ivie said pointedly, stepping between them. "Austin, this is Luolan. Luolan, this is my brother Austin. He's in high school."

We exchanged greetings. Then Olivia gestured for me to come with her. "Come on, Luolan. We should go back."

I nodded and we said our goodbyes. Olivia turned red as a tomato when Austin said goodbye to her, turning away quickly.

"So, what's it with live in tent?" I asked Olivia.

"Ivie's father lost his job a few months ago," Olivia explained. "Their house is rented, and since they couldn't pay the rent, they had to move out. But Ivie's uncle works at the campsite, so he lets them stay here in exchange for a small amount of the money that Ivie's mom makes working at a coffee shop."

"Oh..." I felt bad for Ivie and Austin, having to live in a tent, with no technology. "How they communicate with other people, then?"

"They still have internet. But sometimes it doesn't work."

"Wow."

"I know, right?"

When we reached our campground, Olivia and I slipped through the flaps of our tent and climbed into our sleeping bags. It was about five in the morning and our parents and Ge Ge weren't up yet. But Haiqing apparently was. Or maybe we had woken her when we snuck out for just before I fell asleep, I noticed Haiqing staring at me, an expression of hurt and disbelief plastered on her face.

The next morning, I was looking over my list and checking off items. 1. Make three new friends. Check. 2. Learn English. Almost. 3. Get people to like me. Check. 4. Find a reason to call America 'home'. Suddenly, I heard footsteps behind me. It was Haiqing.

"Luolan?" she asked. "I need to ask you something."

"Yeah?" I replied, not turning away from my list.

"Luolan!" Haiqing cried, with such force that I stepped back. "Luolan, please, listen."

"Okay! I'm listening."

"Last night you snuck out of the tent with Olivia, right?"

"Erm . . . yes?"

"Why didn't you tell me?"

"Well, you see, it really wasn't my decision," I tried to explain. But Haiqing didn't listen.

"Luolan, you've been hanging out with Olivia way more than you hang out with me," she said, frowning. "Are you better friends with her than me or something? You can tell me, you know. It doesn't matter."

For some reason, those words made me so mad. She'd been gushing about Ziwei all the time, and we could never have fun. Why couldn't I talk with Olivia anyway? Haiqing didn't get to choose who I hung out with!

"But always you seem like you don't want to hang out with me!" I cried. "You always talk about Ziwei. If you like her so much, then just go play with her. Be *her* friend; I don't care!" I was practically shouting, all my frustration at Haiqing pouring out all at once.

Then I stopped, realizing what I'd said. I'd basically just told her that I didn't want to be her friend anymore. "Wait, Haiqing..."

"Okay." Haiqing turned away. "If that's what you want, then I will."

"Haiqing..."

"It's fine, Luolan." Haiqing started walking. "I'll leave you with Olivia, then."

Haiqing and her baba left the next day. Olivia didn't ask where they had gone, although she'd probably guessed why already. The rest of us stayed for two more days. Then, on a rainy day that much reflected my mood, we left.

Stop Staring! Yeesh!

Summer passed much too quickly for my taste. Not that I did anything interesting, mind you, but I was really dreading school to start. That's where I would face my doom.

After our camping trip disaster, Haiqing and I didn't email much. She was probably too busy playing with Ziwei. Meanwhile, I babysat Will, wrote on the group newspaper, visited Ivie, teased Ge Ge, and hung out with Olivia. So I take that back. I did lots of interesting things. But they didn't *feel* interesting. My time was taken up worrying about school.

And about Haiqing.

Ge Ge made lots of friends already. He spent his summer playing basketball, trading Pokémon Cards, and flirting with Clara. (One time I caught them together. I teased him nonstop for two weeks.) He seemed to be having fun.

On the first day of the last week of summer, Mama and Baba came to a decision.

"We're taking you kids to do something fun," Mama declared in Chinese. Even though we lived in America now, we still spoke Chinese at home. "Where do you want to go?"

Ge Ge and I looked at each other. *We* came to a united decision.

"Whiz Bang Bong Amusement Park," we said together.

"Where?" Baba asked.

Whiz Bang Bong Amusement Park was a place recommended to us by Clara. We both trusted her judgement and really wanted to go.

"It's an amusement park in Slatertown," Ge Ge replied. "Clara recommended it to us."

"Alright, we can go there," Mama told us.

We grinned. "Thanks, Mama!"

A few minutes later we were loaded in the car. Baba was driving and Mama sat in the front seat so Ge Ge and I were stuck in the back with Ming Ming and his car seat.

We drove for about an hour. When we finally got there, Ge Ge and I practically fell out of the car, trying to climb out.

"Whoa, whoa!" Baba laughed. "No stampeding! You don't want to trample each other!"

Actually, I would've happily trampled Ge Ge to get out of the car and stretch my legs, but I didn't say so. We waited for Baba, Ming Ming, and Mama to get out of the car--much more calmly, of course--and walked inside the gates. Baba bought tickets and Ge Ge and I raced off.

"So which ride do you want to go on first?" I asked Ge Ge. He shrugged.

"The Skydive Dragon," he replied casually. "Why don't you wait here while I go? You can go on something harmless, like . . . hmm . . . the merry-go-round? Perhaps?"

I glared at him. "Be quiet."

"I'm just saying," he replied, ducking a swat to his arm.

I laughed, swatting him again. "Okay, so let's go on the Skydive Dragon."

We walked through the crowd with Ge Ge studying a map, pretending he knew how to read it. He didn't and soon we were hopelessly lost.

As we were trying to find our way back to the entrance so we could find Mama and Baba, I felt someone's eyes on me. I turne, and saw a little boy of about five years old, staring at me, his eyes as big as saucers.

"Mommy," he stage-whispered. "Look, is that Will Baker's babysitter?"

So he was a friend of Will's. I shook my head. If he wanted to whisper, why not do it properly?

"Jare, don't stare," his mother replied, turning him away from me. She shot me an apologetic look.

"But Mommy, why did Will get *that* babysitter?" he whined, pointing at my black hair and almond-shaped eyes. "It makes no sense!"

My face burned red hot. I couldn't move. I felt like someone had dropped a bowling ball on my feet. Did people really think that way about me? That just because I was Chinese I wasn't responsible enough to take care of a five-year-old boy?

"Jaret!" his mother cried, yanking his hand back. "So sorry," she said to me and hurried the boy away.

I glanced at Ge Ge. He obviously overheard the conversation as well. His face was stony and his hands were clenched into fists.

"Come on, Ge Ge," I said quietly. "Let's go find Mama and Baba."

He shook his head. "Eddy warned me that it would be like this in America," he replied quietly. "I didn't believe it until now."

Eddy was one of Ge Ge's new friends.

"Ge Ge, stop," I snapped, knowing I had to get him away so we could find our parents. "It was a five-year-old boy, for heaven's sake. It was just an idiotic comment. So can we go now and just forget about it?"

Ge Ge set his jaw. "Yeah. Yeah, Luolan. You're right. I shouldn't take it so seriously. And Eddy's wrong. It'll be fine."

"That's the spirit!" I punched him again.

"Ow," he complained. "Your bark may be worse than your bite, but you still punch like a pro."

"Ha!" I grinned. "My bark and bite are equally bad. Now let's go. And hey, Ge Ge, the next time you see someone staring at me like that, you say, 'Stop staring! Yeesh!'"

He frowned. "What does 'yeesh' mean?"

"It means that you're annoyed. Imagine the effect it would have."

Ge Ge laughed. "You're funny, Luolan."

"Did you really just notice?"

He laughed. "And what if I did?"

"Then that would be bad."

We wove through the crowd, finally managing to find Mama, Baba, and Ming Ming. Mama taught Ge Ge and me how to read the map properly and soon we were off again, heading toward the Skydive

Dragon. The line was super long, so we decided to wait a few minutes to see if it would lessen.

Ge Ge got some change out of his pocket and bought us a cotton candy each. Then we listened to some musicians play onstage. Ge Ge held his head up high and pretended he was the trumpeter, huffing and puffing into his cotton candy trumpet.

I laughed. "You'd be a terrible trumpeter, Ge Ge."

He pretended to look offended. "I'm sure I'd be marvelous at it."

"Of course."

Ge Ge checked his watch. "It's been thirty minutes," he said. "The line should be shorter now."

In fact, the line was only ten minutes long. Before we knew it, Ge Ge and I were seated in the back of one of the cars.

"Here we go," I cried in excitement as the car began to move.

Just to comment, the Skydive Dragon was not very skydive-y. It just had a few minor drops and a sudden major one that sent everyone into shrieks of delighted terror. In just a few minutes, it was over.

Ge Ge and I came stumbling out, dizzy and disappointed.

"I thought it would be longer," Ge Ge complained.

"And I thought it would be more exciting," I added.

"Let's go on another ride," Ge Ge suggested.

So we did. We went on Power Float (a water ride that soaked us from head to toe), Racetrack (with Ge Ge and me arguing over who got to drive the car. Eventually we just went two times), and Moonwalk (where you go on a tour of the moon from the point of view of a rocketship). Then we played some arcade games, with me winning a stuffed manatee, and Ge Ge winning a doll.

When I saw the doll, I broke down laughing. "Wow," I cried. "I didn't know you played with dolls, Ge Ge!"

Ge Ge scowled. "I was going for the cards, but my hand slipped and the grabber ended up grabbing this thing."

"You should give it to Ming Ming. I bet he'd love it."

Ge Ge laughed. "He'd probably rip its head off and decorate it to look like a decapitated zombie."

"He would never do that!"

"You can never be too certain."

I laughed. "Come on. Mama told us to be back at five."

We strode through the crowd, found our parents, and climbed into the car. Ge Ge tried to give the doll to Ming Ming. It didn't go well.

"Just play with it for one day," Ge Ge pleaded. "Just one short day? If you don't like it at the end of that day, then you can destroy it and turn it into a zombie."

"I don't wanna turn it into a zombie," Ming Ming cried. "I don't like creepy stuff! *Wo bu yao!*"

I shot Ge Ge a look that said, 'I told you so,' and he stuck his tongue out at me.

"Just one day?" I asked Ming Ming, joining in. "Just twenty-four hours!"

"No!"

"Half a day?"

"No!"

"A quarter of a day?"

"No."

"Are you ever gonna agree to this?"

"No."

"I thought so."

Finally, Ge Ge and I rendered the argument hopeless. Ge Ge wanted to burn the doll, but Mama said it would smell terrible. Besides, Ge Ge would more likely burn himself than the doll. In the end, we agreed that Ge Ge would store the doll in the back corner of his closet and never look at it again.

It had been a very exciting day. I almost forgot about Haiqing and Jaret, the boy who spoke rudely about me behind my back. But at night, when I lay down to sleep, the memories came flooding back.

I had known that life in America would be difficult at first. But I hadn't imagined that I would lose my best friend, too.

I pulled out my list. The remaining items on it were: Learn English and Find a Reason to Call America Home. So far, America was as far from home as it could be, and learning English was the least of my worries.

I lay down and slept.

An Encounter in the Mall

It was the day. The day where Mama was going to go nuts in the mall, shopping, shopping, and shopping some more for our school stuff. The day where Ge Ge and I would be tortured beyond measure.

"It's the daaay," I sang, galloping into Ge Ge's room, now covered in gray wallpaper. "Come on, Ge Ge! Let's have it up and comin', up and comin'!"

"Arghh..." Ge Ge groaned. "It's only--" He glanced at his clock. "Eleven in the morning. Let me sleep!"

I laughed. "*Only* eleven in the morning? Wow Ge Ge, when do you want to wake up, four in the afternoon?"

"Exactly!"

Nevertheless, I managed to get Ge Ge out of bed. We ate breakfast and a few minutes later were loaded into the car.

"Are you sure we have to go?" Ge Ge whined. "We could just shop online."

"Some of the things they have in stores they don't have online," Mama explained. "Besides, we're going clothes shopping. You'll need to try stuff on."

"Clothes shopping???"

I covered my ears. "Yowch! It's a small space, Ge Ge. Keep your voice down!"

"Not my favorite thing."

"I can tell."

"Ge Ge Jie Jie fighting," Ming Ming said gleefully. 'Jie Jie', or 'big sister', was what he called me.

"We are not," Ge Ge replied.

"Fighting fighting fighting fighting fighting," Ming Ming sang, covering his ears.

I grinned. "Good luck with that, Ge Ge."

He sighed. "Younger siblings," he muttered. "Who invented them?"

Pretty soon we were at the mall. Baba parked the car then announced he was going to go look at pots and pans in the culinary store.

"Ming Ming wants to come with me," he added. "Don't you, Ming Ming?"

"Fighting fighting fight fight fighting," Ming Ming replied.

"That's so unfair," Ge Ge cried. "How come Ming Ming gets to go with you, but Luolan and I are stuck clothes shopping?"

"Because you need clothes for school," Baba replied patiently. "And you also need school supplies. Ming Ming and I don't."

Ge Ge sighed. "Fine. I guess that makes sense."

I wanted to protest that Mama didn't need school supplies, so why couldn't we just go shopping alone? It was probably because she didn't trust us not to just go to the toy store or something. She was right. That was probably what we would do if left on our own. But I kept quiet. It wouldn't affect her in any way.

"Okay, kids," Mama cried gleefully. "Let's go!"

I groaned and looked at Ge Ge. "Okay. Here goes."

First, we went to the stationary store. That was okay. Then, after we went to the clothes shop, things got bad. Then they got worse. So . . . there was a long line at the checkout counter and we had to wait for about an hour. Then, there was meeting Rennie.

We stopped for lunch in the mall dining hall. Ge Ge and I were waiting in the checkout line when the girl in front of us turned around and spoke.

"Hi," she announced brightly. "I'm Rennie. Rennie Ball."

We both waved and she smiled sympathetically.

"Oh, you don't speak English?" she asked. "It's fine. I take Mandarin class at school." She began speaking with a terrible Chinese accent.

I was about to protest that we did speak English, and we spoke it rather well--we both had been practicing--but Rennie kept on talking. By now, I knew I didn't like her very much.

"Icicle turtles bonked into the cow," she continued, trying to say something in Chinese, but ending up saying this instead.

"Whoa, whoa, whoa!" Ge Ge held up his hand as a gesture for her to stop. "We speak English. We can understand perfectly."

"Oops!" Rennie looked mildly embarrassed. "Silly me! Well! I thought you didn't speak English."

"It was rude," I responded.

"Oh?" Rennie looked surprised, as if she'd forgotten I was there. "I was just assuming, I mean, you looked like you only spoke Chinese."

Ge Ge and I frowned at her. "That makes no sense," Ge Ge replied crossly. "How do we 'look' like we only speak Chinese?"

"Renalda!" a high-pitched voice called.

"Coming, Mother!" Rennie replied. Then to us, "Bye!"

Ge Ge leaned on a shelf. "That is just plain rude. How can she say those things?"

I sighed. "Dunno. Some people are just like that, I guess." Then, it was our turn at the checkout counter and we had to abandon our conversation.

That night, after I practiced my cello, I lay on my bed and thought about what Rennie told us. 'You look like you only spoke Chinese.'

Was it true? Could it be so hard to fit into a new country? Despite my best efforts, people just didn't seem to accept me for who I was. Sure, Clara and Will and Olivia and Ivie all accepted me, but I didn't want them to be the only ones. I didn't want to have to crawl to them for help for the rest of my life.

My journal! I jumped up. I had forgotten about my journal ever since we moved to America. In China, my friends and I had been keeping journals together, writing down our feelings and stuff. I guess I always found it sort of embarrassing, but now it seemed like the perfect thing to express my thoughts on. I got it out of my drawer and wrote, carefully, with the calligraphy brush Haiqing gave me before we moved:

> Everything is happening so fast. I can't keep track of it. Everyone is being weird towards me, and I honestly don't know why. Is this what it will be like at school? I sincerely hope not. All of this on

top of Haiqing? Well, it feels like my brain is going to explode. School is next week. I'm gonna die.

Little did I know that, millions of miles away, on the other side of the world, Haiqing was also writing this in her diary:

I don't know what to do. Without Luolan I'm lonely, but whenever I pick up the phone to call her, or start to type her a message, I don't know what to say. At least I don't think so. I suppose it's also my fault, since I left the camping trip early. Argh! I wonder how Luolan is doing. I really do miss her.

I sighed. Why was life so complicated? Down the hall I could hear Ming Ming crying for his stuffed pig. If only my greatest worries were as simple as Ming Ming's. I lay down and tried to sleep, but I couldn't. Finally, I gave up and tiptoed into Ge Ge's room.

"Ge Ge?" I asked.

"Mmph."

"Aren't you bothered at all by what Rennie said today?"

He rolled over so he was facing me. "Luolan, remember that day at the amusement park when you told me to calm down about that little boy?"

I nodded. "Yeah."

"Well, one thing I've learned since then is that it doesn't matter what other people say. You're you and you'll always be you and there's no point in changing yourself for other people."

"That's not what I was-" I began. He held up a hand.

"Don't get upset over people who aren't worth your time, Luolan," he continued. "And don't waste time worrying about them. Rennie said some ridiculous things. So what? It doesn't matter. She's not worth your time."

"Great speech," I muttered, but inside I knew he was right. Rennie wasn't worth worrying about. She didn't matter.

"Be quiet," Ge Ge laughed. "Now shoo. Go away and don't bother me again."

That sounded more like the Ge Ge I knew. I smiled to myself and exited the room.

Another Fight

The dreaded day had come. I knew it right before I opened my eyes. *Oh no,* I thought as I climbed out of bed. *Oh no,* I thought as I got dressed. *Oh no,* I thought as I brushed my teeth. *Oh*--well, I think you get the idea.

I met up with Ge Ge at the top of the staircase. He was dressed in a pink shirt that Mama bought for him on our shopping mall trip and he looked absolutely ridiculous. I was wearing a blue short sleeve shirt with a pearly white swan embroidered on the front, black shorts, and a braided bracelet I had made back in China. My hair was in a low ponytail and my bangs were shiny and smooth under the light.

"You nervous?" I asked Ge Ge.

"Of course I'm not," he answered. Then he sighed. "Actually, I am. Very. You?"

"I think you know the answer."

"*Dui.*"

We walked down the stairs together then strode into the kitchen where Mama was making pancakes.

"A traditional American breakfast for the first day of school," she said with a laugh.

I smiled, but inside I was disappointed. I had hoped to have *you tiao*, Chinese fried dough, which I always had on the first day of school. It was a family tradition.

We sat down to our breakfasts. After we finished, we packed our lunches. Ge Ge packed chicken nuggets and I packed macaroni and cheese. We bought them at the grocery store and were anxious to taste them. For dessert, we each got a package of Oreos.

As we stepped out of the house, Mama called, "Have a nice day!"

Yeah right. As if that were going to happen. In China, right about now, I would be walking to school with Haiqing, making faces at Dongqiang Zhang and making up impossible tongue twisters we would try out on other people when we got to school. I sighed. And now Haiqing was probably doing all those things with Ziwei, not even missing me.

"Luolan?" Ge Ge called, "You coming?"

I tried to put on a confident face. "Of course I am! I'll race you!"

We got to the bus stop just in time to see the big yellow vehicle rumbling down the street. I'd read about school buses in books, but I'd never seen one before. In China, all the kids either walked or drove in cars to school.

I saw a flash of curly brown hair and Olivia waving to me, Ivie standing beside her.

"Luolan," Olivia squealed. "You're here! I was waiting for you!"

I laughed. "Hey, Olivia! Hi, Ivie!"

"I seriously can't believe that we're actually going to school together!" Olivia exclaimed. "Let me introduce you to everyone." She gestured to a girl standing in the corner. "That's Rennie, and she—"

My heart sank to the tips of my toes. "Rennie? She's here?"

"Of course," Olivia knit her brows. "Have you met?"

"Erm..."

Just then, Rennie stepped over. "Oh, hey," she said. "You're the Chinese girl I met in the shopping mall, right?" She turned to Ge Ge. "And I met you too! How exciting!"

"Rennie, these are Luolan and Lizhong," Ivie introduced us. "Luolan'll be in sixth grade with us."

"How do you do?" Rennie asked us. Then, "My mommy always taught me to be polite."

"Polite?" Ge Ge muttered under his breath. "Huh."

I grinned at him.

"Come on, kids," the bus driver hollered. "Don't wanna be late!"

Ge Ge and I climbed onto the bus. He sat in the back with all the other seventh graders. Inside, it was musty and smelled like day-old cheese. I held my nose.

"What's wrong?" Ivie asked.

"The bus smells," I replied.

She laughed. "You'll get used to it. We all do sometime or another. Most of us have been taking the bus since kindergarten."

I guessed that her words were meant to reassure me, but they did the exact opposite of that. Since *kindergarten?* These kids had known each other for so long. How could I ever fit in?

The bus rumbled down the corner, stopping to pick up a bunch of other kids. We drove for a few more minutes, then got stuck in traffic.

"Ugh!" Rennie groaned. "Construction."

"Weren't they supposed to be done yesterday?" the blond girl who sat next to her asked.

"I know! So irresponsible!" Rennie tossed her hair. "Come on, Catherine, let's play Avocado." She glanced at me and smirked, like, *Oh, poor Luolan. You don't have any friends? Too bad, because I do.*

"Don't pay any attention to them," Ivie told me, touching my arm. "Catherine and Rennie are nincompoops."

"Nincompoops?"

"Weird, bothersome," Olivia supplied, laughing. "They're super annoying. Tyra, too. She's a girl in seventh grade. But you won't have to worry about her, since she's a grade higher."

"My brother in seventh grade."

"Oh," Ivie shrugged. "Poor him."

"I heard the seventh grade English teacher eats kids for breakfast," Olivia whispered in a spooky voice. "And then drinks their blood and turns their guts into bracelets."

"My gosh, Olivia," Ivie shrieked with delight. "That is sooo gross."

I screamed. "Oh no! I am wearing a bracelet! Maybe it is made out of guts."

We broke down laughing.

"Yo, be quiet back there," the bus driver hollered.

Olivia made a face. "That's Mr. Stevie," she explained. "He never lets us kids have any fun."

"You must sit down right now or you'll get detention!" Ivie said, doing her imitation of Mr. Stevie.

"What detention?" I asked.

"It's basically what you get if you do something bad," Olivia explained. "You have to stay after school and do homework. If you get three detentions, then you can't run for student council."

"Student council?"

"The group of kids who get to make decisions for the school. There are six people, two from each grade. Last year, Ivie was one of the people."

Ivie blushed. "It's super fun," she said. "You get to change stuff. Plus, you get to miss classes for meetings."

"Sounds cool." It didn't sound all that appealing to me, but I said it to be polite.

"Okay, kids, get out, get out," Mr. Stevie called. We were at Andrew Jackson Middle School.

"Hey, that reminds me," Olivia said to Ivie. "Is Austin at school today?"

Ivie winked at me. "He's sick."

"Sick on the first day of school?" Olivia asked sympathetically. "Poor guy."

"Kidding!" Ivie cried gleefully. "He's in high school, remember? He takes a different bus from us."

Olivia stuck her tongue out. "You're so mean!"

"Thanks."

"So, who is our teacher?" I asked, attempting to change the subject. It worked.

"We'll each all have a lot of different teachers," Ivie told me. "For instance, there are two math teachers, three P.E. teachers, and a couple of music teachers. I think. I'm pretty sure."

"Let's go inside and see," Olivia suggested. We all agreed to that.

Inside the school, Ivie and Olivia both made a beeline for the main office to get their schedules. I followed, since I also needed to get mine.

"Hello, girls," the woman behind the desk said to us. She had frizzy red hair, hot pink glasses, and a nice smile. "Come to get your schedules? By the way, I'm Mrs. Shorter, the secretary. You can come to me if you need anything or you left your homework on the bus or you want to quit school and call your parents to pick you up." She laughed, and I could tell she was joking. "That hardly ever happens, but you never know." She winked. "Now, may I take your names?"

We introduced ourselves, and she clicked her tongue. "Nice names. Now . . . Luolan Xia, right?" she asked me. I nodded, and she opened a drawer, muttering, "Luolan Luolan Luolan . . . Oh! There you are!" She handed me a blue folder. "You'll find your schedule, the lunch menu, and a map of the school in there. But I hardly think you'll need it. It's not a very big place and even if you do get lost, there's always plenty of nice people to help you find your way."

I smiled and thanked her. Mrs. Shorter gave folders to Olivia and Ivie and soon we were off again.

"So, what are your first classes?" Ivie asked Olivia and me.

"I have homeroom with Mrs. McReddy and then I'm staying there for science," Olivia replied.

"What about you, Luolan?" Ivie asked me.

"I have homeroom with Mrs. McReddy, too!" I exclaimed, scanning my schedule. Then my face fell. "But then have English with Ms. Cahn."

Olivia patted my shoulder. "But we have theater together after lunch, remember?" She pointed to a green square on my schedule. "And so does Ivie."

"You doing theater, too?" I asked Ivie. She nodded.

"I have homeroom with you guys, but then I'm going to health with Mrs. Hendall." She sighed. "I hate health. Well, come on. Don't want to be late."

We put our arms around each other and trudged toward homeroom. And at that moment, I felt great. Like we were a team.

"Hey, that's the girl who stood up at the beginning of class," someone behind me snickered. "Yo, kid, what's up with the American food? Thought you were supposed to have dumplings or somethin'!"

I groaned. Why wouldn't he leave me alone? Just because of the incident had happened at the beginning of homeroom, doesn't mean he had to torment me for a lifetime. I shut my eyes, remembering.

Ivie, Olivia, and I just sat down at our desks for homeroom when the teacher came in. I stood up, just as I had back in China. Someone giggled behind me and I realized no one else was standing. With a sinking feeling in my chest, I sat.

"Um, okay..." Mrs. McReddy said nervously. "So . . . attendance." She pulled a clipboard from her desk and started reading names. "Ivalyn Anderbell?"

"Here. Please call me Ivie."

"Okay, Ivie. Ethan Arnold?"

"Here," a nervous-looking boy with curly blond hair spoke up from the back of the room.

"Ellie Azalea?"

"Here," said a short brunette to my left.

"Renalda Ball?"

I jumped, looking around. Rennie? She was in my homeroom? Oh no. This couldn't be happening.

"Here. Please call me Rennie." Rennie smiled a winning smile. "You have *such* a pretty headband."

I glanced at Mrs. McReddy's headband. It was downright ugly. But Mrs. McReddy smiled like she'd just won the lottery. "Why, thank you, dear. I quite like it myself."

The teacher called a few more names. Then she came to my name. "Lu--er Lola? Is it Lola?"

"Luolan Xia," I said, standing up. "*Dao*. I mean, um, here."

"Sit down," Rennie hissed. "Stop embarrassing yourself."

My face burned fire hot. I sat down and buried my face in my hands. Ivie patted my back. I couldn't wait for the day to end.

I stepped out of the memory. I turned and glared at the boy who had just made fun of me. Before I could say anything, Olivia jumped in.

"Be quiet, Donny," she snapped. "Your dad is Irish. So if Luolan has to have a Chinese meal, then shouldn't you have an Irish one?" She glared at him until he turned away, muttering.

"Good one," Ivie laughed, patting Olivia on the back.

I was quiet. I didn't like Olivia fighting my battles for me. And now some of the girls from the other tables were looking at me and giggling, making attempts to hide their smiles. Rennie, Catherine, and Ellie Azalea, the girl from my homeroom. I turned away.

"Hey, Luolan," Ivie said over to me. "Are you okay?"

I didn't respond and continued eating my sandwich.

"Um . . . Luolan?"

I was silent for the rest of lunch. And when they tried talking to me on the bus, I turned away. I didn't know why I was annoyed. I just was. So much for feeling like a team.

Bing! my phone cried cheerfully, signifying I had a text. I sighed, rolled over and picked up my phone. My annoyance of being interrupted from my book vanished when I saw that it was Olivia.

I learned shorthand from Ivie, who insisted on teaching me the basics of not taking up too much time while texting. I had it down now and was excited to test my knowledge. I read Olivia's message:

Olivia: What happened 2day? R u ok?

I hesitated, wondering what to do. Finally, I responded.

Luolan: Am fine.
Olivia: R u sure?
Luolan: Yeah
Olivia: Then what happened 2day at lunch?
Luolan: Nothing
Olivia: Could've fooled me
Luolan: just don't like people fighting battles 4 me, ok?
Olivia: Oh. You could've just told me, u know
Luolan: I know

Olivia: I just don't like people picking on my friends

Luolan: Yeah

Olivia: Donny O'Sullivan is an idiot

Luolan: That means . . . o right :D

Olivia: Don't let him bother u

Luolan: OK. Next time see him, say "stop staring! Yeesh!"

Olivia: Hahaha :) That'll shut him up. Cya tmrw

Luolan: Bye

I turned off my phone, feeling happy. At least I had made up with one friend. Then I remembered Haiqing. What could I do about her? Gathering my courage, I turned my phone on again.

Luolan: Haiqing? You there?

No response. I sighed and forged ahead.

Luolan: Well, anyway. Haiqing, I'm so sorry for sneaking out with Olivia and spending more time with her than with you. I really shouldn't have said what I said. If you get this, please reply. I'm super sorry, and I really hope that you can come back for a sleepover. Bye.

I turned off my phone. Nothing I could do now but wait.

Writing Club

Days passed. School became more bearable. I still studied English with Ge Ge, though. My grammar was getting better, but I still didn't know a lot of big words and I couldn't get the accent right.

Oh well, I'd get there. Ge Ge and I drilled each other with flashcards at least once a week.

Mr. and Mrs. Baker recommended me to one of their neighbors, the Wilkinsons. They asked me to babysit their six-year-old twins, Elias and Ella. I agreed. When I got there, Elias and Ella were in the playroom, playing Destroy the Castle with Ella as the castle and Elias as the destroyer. They played for a whole hour. Then they started coloring. It wasn't a hard job. Plus, I got fifteen dollars to pay for a new book I desperately wanted.

One sunny Monday, I was walking down the hall to theater class when I spotted a flyer on the bulletin board.

Come join the
Andrew Jackson Middle School Writing Club!

- **Great fun!**
- **Wild adventures! (in your stories)**
- **Hanging out with friends!**

Meets after school on Mon., Tue., and Fri. from 3:30 PM-4:30 PM in the seventh grade history room, starting September 16th. See Skylar Byrne (7th grade) for details.

Below was the sign-up sheet. I hesitated, then wrote my name on it. I smiled to myself. Today was September 16th. Awesome.

After the final bell rang, I headed downstairs to the history room for the first meeting.

I took a deep breath, then turned the doorknob. Inside were about ten to fifteen kids. They all turned and stared as I came in. I blushed and sat down at an empty desk.

"Hey," said a guy with a sparkly silver watch. I recognized him as Ethan Arnold, the guy from homeroom that always sat in the back.

"Hi," I replied. "You're Ethan?"

"Um, yeah. You're Luolan?"

I nodded, pleased that he had gotten my name right.

"Well, I saw your drawings in science class. They were really good."

"Thanks." I was too embarrassed to admit I'd never noticed him in science before. I absently fiddled with a lock of black hair, smoothing it back into my ponytail. "No one's ever complimented me on my drawings before."

"Well, I don't see why not." Ethan held my gaze a little longer before looking at the floor. "Well, see you around, Luolan."

It took me a moment to figure out who he was talking to: me, or the floor. By the time I figured it out, he had slipped away. I didn't have time to process what just happened because a girl with reddish golden-brown hair and hazel eyes stepped to the front of the room.

"Okay guys." She raised her hands for silence. "I'm Skylar Byrne. I'm in seventh grade. Welcome to the writing club. So, first order of business. We need to think of a name for our club. Does anyone have any ideas?"

"The Pusheens," someone called out.

Skylar frowned. "No . . . something to do with writing."

"The Writers!"

"Too obvious."

"The Evil Storytellers!"

"Too random."

"The Young Authors Group!"

"Too boring."

Skylar looked around. "Any more ideas?" When no one responded, she sighed. "Well, if anyone has an idea, just tell me. Or something. So anyway, we're going to do a big writing project. About something. I don't know yet. So anyway, if you guys could get into partners and discuss what topic you want to do it about, that would be great. For me,

I guess. Dunno about you." We all laughed. Skylar waved her hands. "Shoo! Shoo!"

Everyone scrambled to find partners. Soon, pretty much everyone was paired up except for Ethan, me, and two other kids from seventh grade I didn't know. The seventh graders quickly paired up and sat down at a desk together, so Ethan and I had to pair up. We sat at a desk together and began discussing topic ideas.

"So . . . maybe the world?" Ethan suggested.

"But that is too big a topic," I replied. "How about we move down to one or two continents?"

Ethan obliged. "North America?"

"How about Asia?"

"North America and Asia."

We agreed on that. Suddenly, I was struck with a brilliant idea. "Moving!" I cried, making people around me cringe and cover their ears. "Moving from one continent to another, like I did!"

Ethan grinned, covering his ears. "That's brilliant!"

I smiled. "I know I am."

"You are." I could tell he meant it. Genuinely.

"Um, what kind of project should we do?" I asked, clearing my throat.

"Maybe everyone could write something," he replied. "And we could display it somewhere."

"Oh, yeah!" I cried, warming up to his idea. "Maybe we can ask teachers if we could have a night when all the parents come and we could do a talk, and--"

"Whoa whoa whoa," Ethan said, laughing. "That's a good idea, but we have to talk to Skylar first. We haven't even been selected, remember?"

I blushed. "Oops. Yes, you're right."

"But it is a good idea."

"Thanks."

"Okay, guys," Skylar called. "We'll have each group come up and present their idea. Who wants to go first?"

Our hands shot into the air and Skylar called on us. We stood up nervously.

"Um, so we were thinking of doing a writing project on moving," Ethan explained. "Based on Luolan's experiences moving from China to America."

"You moved from China to America?" a kid in the back row asked. "How cool is that?"

"Can you tell us more about it sometime?" a girl sitting in front of me asked.

"Sure!"

"You should write a story about it," a boy with a Red Sox cap told me.

"I just might."

"Back to the topic," Skylar called. "Ethan?"

Ethan smiled at her. "So, anyway, we were thinking . . . well, Luolan was, anyway, that we could do an exhibition or something, and ask all the parents to come. Each of us could do a different thing that has to do with writing. We put them all together, and poof, we have a project!" We sat down again.

Skylar grinned at us. "Cool. Next?"

Once everyone had gone, we voted again. We won.

On the way out of school, Ethan caught up to me. "Hey, Luolan," he said. "Nice job with the idea."

I smiled shyly. "Thanks. You came up with the subject, though."

"Well, yeah." He grinned. "I know, I'm smart." We both laughed. "See you tomorrow, Luolan," Ethan said.

"Yeah, tomorrow," I echoed. He waved. I waved back. Then he was gone.

"Aww, looks like someone's got a bo-oy-frien-end," a voice sang in my ear. I turned and groaned. It was Rennie. "Who is he?" Rennie asked, circling me. "You like him, don't you? Does he like you back? Do you know? Ooooh!"

I sighed. "Rennie, stay out of my business. How did you get here?"

"Soccer practice." Rennie pouted. "But I love these kinds of juicy gossip! Please do tell? Just a bit? Hey, Cat, come listen! Lolan's got a boyfriend!"

Catherine, the girl from the bus, came waltzing over just as I was saying, "My name is Luolan. Not Lolan."

"Oh?" Rennie cocked her head, pretending to listen. "Ulan? Okay, Ulan. Cat, this is Ulan. Ulan, this is Cat. You haven't officially met, have you?"

Cat shook her head dutifully. "Hi Ulan! I'm Catherine Hart. But you can call me Cat. C-A-T. Like the animal. Do you know what that means?"

"I do," I hissed between gritted teeth. "I am not an idiot." I was proud to finally be able to put that word to good use.

Cat recoiled. "Gee, I'm sorry."

"So stop staring! Yeesh!" I whirled and marched out of the school, my head held high, leaving two very stunned people behind me.

On the late bus home, I sat in a seat alone. Ethan wasn't on my bus so I couldn't even talk to him. So I turned on my phone and checked my phone. No reply from Haiqing. Ugh. So I texted Olivia.

Luolan:	Hey, Olivia!
Olivia:	Hi! What's up?
Luolan:	Am on late bus from writing club
Olivia:	Cool! Wut did u do?
Luolan:	I met a kid, Ethan Arnold
Olivia:	You mean that guy from homeroom?
Luolan:	Yea
Olivia:	How'd u meet him?
Luolan:	So first he complimented me on my artwork, and then we paired up at writing club . . . .then complimented me again before left...
Olivia:	O MY GOSH
Luolan:	Wut
Olivia:	Awwwww! Luolan, he likes you!
Luolan:	EXCUSE ME???!!!!
Olivia:	This is soooooo cute.......!
Luolan:	I'm getting off
Olivia:	K. Come 2 my house, OK?
Luolan:	Sure. Bye

Ethan. Liked me. Luolan. According to Olivia, at least. And she was not the most reliable source. But if she was right...Oh my. The bus rolled to a stop in front of my house, and I got off.

"Hey, Mama! I'm home," I called as I opened the door.

"Hey, Luolan! I wasn't expecting you so late," Mama cried, coming down the stairs. "I got your text about going to the writing club. How was it?"

"Awesome." I put my backpack down and ran upstairs. "Ge Ge," I called. "Hey!"

Ge Ge came out of his now-black-wallpapered room, covering his ears with his shirt. His hands were covered with icky purple jello. "What?" he asked, irritated. "I was doing a very important science experiment!"

"Sorry," I replied, even though I wasn't. "You know that girl you liked back in China? What was her name? Yin something something?"

"Yin Meng Yao," Ge Ge said. "Yeah. What about her?"

"What did you do to get her to like you back?" I asked. "Did you give her anything? Or say anything?"

"I didn't do anything," Ge Ge replied haughtily. "I admired her from afar. Got a problem with that?"

I hid my smile. "Of course not, Ge Ge." He was going to be no help. So I used the only option that I had left. I went to Olivia's.

The Land of the Free

"For last time, Olivia, he NOT likes me," I cried. She grinned.

"Are you sure?" Olivia's eyes danced. "Tell me what he said."

"But I already told you many times," I protested. "Just give me final decision!"

"Don't you worry." Olivia laughed. "'Cause Olivia knows all."

"What kind of logic is that?" I complained.

"It's not. It's a fact."

I sighed. "I better go now. Tell me when figure it out, okay?"

"I already have."

"What is it?"

"He likes you."

I groaned. "Fine. I am going now."

"Bye!"

I shut Olivia's front door as gently as I could behind me, for it was old and could easily fall apart. Then I hopped on my bike--which Baba had found at a garage sale and fixed up for me--and sped off toward home.

I opened the door and found Ge Ge and Ming Ming arguing.

"NO MCDONALDS!" Ming Ming was shouting. "NO NO NO!"

Ge Ge looked up wearily. "Oh, Luolan, finally! Maybe you can talk some sense into Ming Ming here."

I raised my hands as a gesture of peace. "Um, what?"

"Ming Ming doesn't want to go out to get fast food."

"NO MCDONALDS!"

"Ming Ming, you like McDonalds, remember?" I coaxed. "We had McDonalds on our first day here!" I turned to Ge Ge. "Um, why do we want to go to McDonalds?"

"Mama's out shopping and Baba is meeting with his customers," Ge Ge replied under his breath. "I'm hungry, and there's nothing good in the fridge."

"By 'nothing good', do you mean 'nothing unhealthy'?" I teased.

He rolled his eyes. "Fine, yes. Please help me."

"Come on, Ming Ming," I pleaded, using my most convincing voice. "They have fried dough..." That was his one weakness. Ming Ming *loved* fried dough, even though it wasn't good for him.

Ming Ming hesitated. Ge Ge gave me the thumbs-up sign behind his back. "Okay," Ming Ming relented. "I go McDonalds."

Ge Ge high-fived me. "Great! Let's go. It's just a few blocks away."

Yay me. I got Ming Ming to come to McDonalds and in return, Ge Ge made me carry him. Of course, Ming Ming was perfectly capable of walking, but he *had* to insist that someone carry him. Yay. Just yay.

"*Wo men dao le ma?* Are we there yet?" I panted, stopping to catch my breath.

"Just a few more minutes," Ge Ge said cheerfully. Easy for him to say. He wasn't the one with a thirty pound toddler on his back.

Finally, we reached McDonalds. I set Ming Ming down in front of the door. "No!" he wailed. "Luolan carry me!"

"Get Ge Ge to carry you," I replied, breathing heavily. "I'm not carrying you any farther."

So Ge Ge ended up having to carry Ming Ming inside McDonalds and through the checkout line. Ahhh. Revenge was sweet.

After we got our food, we sat outside to eat. Ming Ming sat in Ge Ge's lap, bouncing happily as he ate his sandwich, blissfully ignoring Ge Ge's grumbles of pain.

"It's--Ow, Ming Ming, stop it!-- so hot today!" Ge Ge exclaimed, fanning his face. "After we eat, do you wanna go get some ice cream?"

"You mean the ice cream at McDonalds? I think they only have two flavors."

"No," Ge Ge replied, a mischievous glint in his eyes. "I mean, the ice cream across the street, at the Cold Cold Ice Cream Shoppe."

I stared at him. "Do you think Mama would let us?"

He shook his head. "Nope. But it's America! The Land of the Free! We're free to do whatever we like."

I didn't think that was how it worked, but I didn't contradict. Besides, I wanted an ice cream. "What do you think, Ming Ming?" I asked. "Should we?"

Ming Ming nodded vigorously. Ge Ge grinned at me. "I think that's a yes. Don't you?"

I laughed. "Lead on, big brother."

As we entered the Cold Cold Ice Cream Shoppe, we felt a blast of cold air hit us like snowballs. Ge Ge practically collapsed on the counter.

"Ge Ge," I said, nudging him. "We're in public, stop it!'

"Ugh," he groaned. "But I'm soooo hoooooott."

"Aren't we all. Look, there's so many ice cream flavors!" I pointed to the display case. That got his attention.

"Oh, wow! Luolan, come look! There's mint chocolate chip and Fudgsicle-- whatever that is--and cookie dough, and lemon sorbet," Ge Ge breathed. Oh, one thing to mention, my brother is a *huge* food addict.

"Lemon orbaaaaaay!" Ming Ming sang, jumping out of my arms-- yes, I had to carry him AGAIN--and waltzed over to the case.

"It's SORbet," Ge Ge tried to teach him, emphasizing the "sor" in sorbet.

"Orbay orbay orbayyyyyyyy!"

"Ugh," Ge Ge groaned. "He'll never learn."

"He's only two," I reminded him. "Sometimes you treat him like a six-year-old."

"Sometimes he's as *annoying* as a six-year-old," Ge Ge grumbled.

Suddenly, I heard snickering behind me. I turned and saw two girls laughing and pointing at me. Rennie and Cat.

"Ugh," I groaned. "Won't they just leave me alone for once?"

"Who?" Ge Ge asked, now on high alert. He followed my gaze. "Rennie?! It seems like everywhere we go, there she is."

"I know, right?" I asked. "She's soooo annoying!"

"Hey," Rennie called from across the room. "Ulan!"

I pretended to ignore her. Ge Ge took Ming Ming by the hand and told him to pick his flavor.

"Ulan, what's up with that shirt?" Rennie asked. "It's so . . . last-season. Ugh."

Cat giggled. "Hi, Ulan! Or was it Lolan?"

They dissolved into giggles.

"Come on, Luolan," Ge Ge said in a low voice. "Pick your flavor."

"I'm not hungry anymore."

"Okay." He and Ming Ming were both holding cones. "If you want any later, I think there's a chocolate bar in the freezer back home." Ge Ge handed the cashier a wad of cash. "Keep the change," he told the cashier, who looked delighted. Then he turned to me. "Now let's go."

We speed-walked out of the shop. As we walked home, my heart felt like it was slowly sinking to the ground. What was Rennie's problem? If this was the Land of the Free, then I wanted to be free of Rennie.

My spirits lifted a bit when we saw a man selling balloons on the street. "Hey," I said to Ming Ming. "Do you want a balloon?"

"Balloon!" he agreed.

"You guys go ahead," I told my siblings. "I know the way. I'll meet you back at our house with the balloon."

I crossed the street and said hi to the man. "Can I have a balloon for little brother, please?" I asked him.

"Sure thing, kid," he replied. He had brown hair and blue eyes with crinkles at the corners that indicated that he smiled a lot. "What's your name?"

"Luolan Xia," I told him, speaking slowly so that he would hear it better.

"Luolan," he repeated perfectly. "Are you Chinese?" I nodded, and he said, "You know, my grandmother was Chinese. Her name was Meilin. My name is Chance."

"Chance?" I asked, before I could stop myself. "Oh sorry, I do not mean to be rude, I--"

Chance laughed. "I know, it's an odd name. But when I was little, my mother would always say, 'Chance, I named you this because I want you to never forget that you have to take chances in life. You haven't truly lived until you've faced your fears, overcome your obstacles, and tried something new.'" Chance gazed wistfully into the distance. "And I never did forget."

"Well, I think a wonderful name."

"Thanks! I like Luolan, too. Here's your balloon." He scribbled something on it and handed the balloon to me. When I started to give him the money, he pushed it back. "No, no. It's for free. Give your little brother my best wishes."

I grinned at him. "Thanks, Chance."

"I hope we meet again, Luolan," Chance said. He tipped his cap toward me. "Until next time, then."

"Until next time," I agreed. Then I turned and crossed the street. When I looked back, Chance was gone.

This is what makes the Land of the Free free, I realized. People like Chance. Like Olivia, and Ivie, and even Ethan. It's just like Ge Ge said. It doesn't matter what Rennie, or Cat, or anyone else thinks or says. People like that don't matter. It's the people who do that count.

I looked at the balloon. It was plain yellow, a sunny color to penetrate my cloudy mood. But when I looked closer, I saw words written in spiky handwriting.

To the Xia family:
Never stop facing your fears
Always take CHANCEs
(Get it? Haha. Lame joke. I know.)
Best of luck in everything
Chance Gold

Chance had left us a message! I wondered what Ge Ge would make of it. My head felt like it would float off my shoulders in happiness as I started making my way home.

The School Play

"Okay, class!" Mr. Caleb, our theater teacher called, clapping his hands together to call us to attention. "Happy Halloween!"

The class cheered. I cheered with them. Ming Ming was going Trick-or-Treating later tonight. He was super excited, for we hadn't had Halloween in China.

Mr. Caleb raised his hands. "Yes, yes, I know, but to add to the excitement, I have news for you."

Olivia, Ivie, and I turned as one, focusing our attention on him. Mr. John Caleb was a short man with leaf green eyes and a brown mustache. He had been a professional actor back in the day, but now he was pursuing a new career and fulfilling his dream of being a teacher. Mr. Caleb had a quiet voice, but when he spoke, everybody listened. He was also very dramatic.

"Over the last few weeks, we have really delved deep into what it means to be a Triple Threat actor," Mr. Caleb told us. "Now, we're going to work on putting on a musical."

Murmurs of excitement wove through the classroom. Olivia squeezed my hand in anticipation.

"So our musical is going to be..." Mr. Caleb drum-rolled dramatically. *"The Little Mermaid!"*

Now the murmurs were of disappointment.

"Now, now," Mr. Caleb laughed. "I know it doesn't sound very appealing. But *The Little Mermaid* is a wonderful musical to do. You guys will love it, I'm sure."

"Like the one they had on Broadway?" a kid asked.

"Yes. Except, I'm the one writing the script. The songs are the same, though."

"That sounds nice."

To contradict that, everyone yawned, including me.

"Guys, this is a wonderful opportunity," Mr. Caleb sighed. "How about I let you listen to one of the songs?" He didn't wait for us to reply before he put on *Part of Your World.*

When the song ended, we were all amazed. "You mean, the girl who plays Ariel gets to sing that?" Ivie asked. Mr. Caleb nodded. "Then I'm in!"

One by one, the other kids all pledged their allegiance to Mr. Caleb. Mr. Caleb looked ready to burst with happiness.

"Okay," the drama teacher rubbed his hands together. "I'll send you the link for auditions. They're next week, so be prepared!"

We all left class feeling determined and happy.

Ethan caught up to me at the end of class. "Hey, Luolan," he said. "How do you think you're gonna do?"

I shrugged. "I don't know! I have never done an audition before!"

Ethan laughed. "Well, good luck."

I smiled. He waved and left. Olivia grinned at me. I ignored her, humming a little tune--'*Part of Your World*,' probably. An image of Ethan was stuck in my head for the rest of the day.

That night, I checked my texts. Haiqing still hadn't responded. What was her problem? Instead, I texted Ivie and Olivia on our group chat.

Luolan:	Hey guys!
Ivie:	Hi!
Olivia:	Wuts up?
Luolan:	Wut part u gonna try out?
Olivia:	King Triton
Ivie:	Ariel
Olivia:	O, you'll get it, Ivie
Ivie:	Wut makes u think that?
Olivia:	Ur such a good singer
Ivie:	Ugh
Olivia:	Wut about you, Luolan?
Luolan:	Ursula
Ivie:	Cool!
Olivia:	Ya think you'll get it?
Luolan:	Don't know. Probably not
Ivie:	Why?
Luolan:	Lots of good actors in class
Olivia:	Like who?
Luolan:	Banana
Olivia:	?
Ivie:	U mean Berecca?

Luolan: Yea, her

Olivia: Haha! Banana

Luolan: She is good. Did u hear when we did voice?

Ivie: She is pretty good

Olivia: Ivie! Way to boost self-esteem!

Ivie: Sry. She is, tho

Luolan: I get ur point

Olivia: I think you'll get the part

Luolan: Thxs

Ivie: I have to go. Swim team practice

Olivia: Bye!

Luolan: Cya

Ivie: Bye

Olivia: I'd better go do homework

Luolan: O. OK. Bye!

Olivia: Bye

I turned off my phone and wrote the last answer to my math homework. Then I turned on my computer and typed into the website for the audition music. I selected one of the songs and music blasted from the computer.

"Yowch!" Ge Ge cried from his room. "That's louder than your voice, Luolan!"

"Sorry!" I turned the music down and took out my math homework. That night, I fell asleep listening to Sebastian singing 'Under the Sea'.

* * *

It was the day of the audition. I met up with Olivia and Ivie before theater.

"Nervous?" Olivia asked us.

Ivie nodded vigorously. I shrugged. "Not really, I practiced every night."

Olivia looked amazed. "I'm the opposite of you. I'm pretty sure I'll die."

I laughed and patted her shoulder. "You'll be fine."

As we entered the room, I could tell something wasn't right. Mr. Caleb wasn't sitting in his black director's chair. Instead, there was a woman of about 50 or 60.

"Hello, girls," she said to us. "I'm Ms. Leonard. Mr. Caleb wasn't able to make it today and he didn't want to postpone the audition, so I'm subbing for him. Are you ready?"

We nodded and smiled, but inside we were all uneasy. Did this teacher know anything about acting? It sure didn't look like it.

"Okay, class," Ms. Leonard called after a few more kids straggled in. "Auditions. I'm not sure I know much about auditions, so you guys will have to help me."

Olivia, Ivie, and I exchanged uneasy glances. We couldn't help her because we were the kids doing the auditions! If Mr. Caleb wanted a substitute, why not get a substitute that at least knew a little about acting?

"So..." Ms. Leonard said. "First up, Ivalyn Anderbell."

Ivie looked at us nervously. I squeezed her hand. That gave her courage. She stood up and sang in her sweet soprano voice, "What would I give to live where you are..." She didn't mess up one time. I noticed Ms. Leonard writing furiously next to her name, a smile on her face.

After Ivie went came Banana--sorry, *Berecca*. She messed up in the middle of her song and collapsed into her seat, crying. Then a bunch of other people auditioned, including Ethan, who sang 'One Step Closer'. One girl, Jacquelyn Ferris, who was auditioning for a mersister, tap-danced across the floor, smiling and waving until Ms. Leonard told her that mermaids probably didn't tap-dance.

Finally, Olivia. She had to restart because she lost her place, but otherwise she was great. After that, a few more people went, including a boy named Dave. He was going for Sebastian and he was good, but he couldn't hit all the high notes. After him . . . me. My heart was threatening to pound out of my chest as I waited for Ms. Leonard to call my name.

"Lu--uh--Loulin?" Ms. Leonard asked. "Is it Loulin?"

"Luolan," I told her, gritting my teeth. "Luolan Xia. My name is Luolan Xia."

"Well, hello. I don't think I've met you before."

I sighed. Hadn't she said hello to me when I just came in? "Why don't you stand up and sing for us, Luolan?"

I stood up. "I am auditioning for Ursula, and I will be singing '*Poor Unfortunate Souls*'."

"Really? You? Don't you think you'd make a better . . . background fish?"

Someone giggled. Olivia was staring at Ms. Leonard like she wanted to murder her.

I stared at her, my face burning. "Excuse me?"

"Well, whatever. Go ahead, Loulin."

So I sang.

"So, how do you think you did?" I asked Ivie and Olivia after the audition.

"Terrible," Olivia muttered. "Did you hear me have to restart?"

"It was pretty bad," Ivie replied under her breath.

"IVIE!" we yelled in unison. Ivie burst out laughing.

"I'm kidding! I'm kidding!"

"Mr. Caleb's posting the cast list on Friday," Olivia said, growing serious. "I'm so nervous."

"Well, even if you don't get your part, you'll still get to do lighting, or costume design, or something," Ivie pointed out.

"But you probably will get it," I reassured her.

"Thanks," Olivia told me.

Ivie took a breath. "Now we just have to wait."

I grinned at her. "I know hate waiting."

Ivie sighed. "Yeah..."

"Is something bothering you?" Olivia asked.

"It's just my parents," Ivie told us. "They've been fighting a lot, and . . . well, I'm afraid that they're going to . . . split up."

"Oh no," I gasped. "Poor you!"

Ivie sighed. "I'm sorry I haven't told you before. There's just been so much going on."

"It's not your fault," Olivia replied.

I nodded. "Even if they do split up, you have us."

Ivie smiled softly. "Thanks." Then, after a moment, she giggled. "You know, this feels so cheesy right now."

Olivia punched her on the shoulder. "Hey, don't contradict our excellent comforting skills."

"But seriously," I put in. "You be fine. We're here."

Ivie just put her arms around us and didn't say anything. But her smile told us everything we needed to know.

Casted! Not So Much

That night, as I lay on my bed, it occurred to me that Haiqing hadn't texted me in a long time. I checked my messages, just to make sure, and sure enough, there wasn't anything. The last time she'd texted was before the camping trip. Where was she? Was she still mad about what happened at the trip? I still regretted what I said big-time.

I rubbed my eyes. I was so tired. I'd gone to sleep late last night because of homework. I just wanted to close my heavy eyelids and relax my mind and dream and....

"Oh no!" was the first thing I said in the morning as soon as I woke up. I desperately grasped around, a feeling of doom settling over me.

The first thing I saw was a folder full of paper with words written all over them. I breathed a sigh of relief. I had done all my homework! Then I looked down at my clothes and groaned. I *hated* falling asleep in my clothes!

I got dressed rapidly and stuffed my homework in my bag. I shoveled down a few spoonfuls of oatmeal and slammed my feet into my shoes. I didn't bother packing a lunch, since I had taken to the cafeteria food.

"Meet you at the bus stop," I hollered over my shoulder to Ge Ge, who was still eating breakfast.

I ran to the bus stop. Olivia was there already. "Hey," I panted. "Is Ivie here yet?"

She shook her head. "No. You look rushed."

"I am," I replied. "I accidentally fell asleep in my clothes yesterday."

"Oh." Olivia sighed and patted my shoulder. "That's the worst."

From the corner of my eye, I saw Ge Ge run to the bus stop. I waved at him and he waved back. I noticed he was still holding an apple in his hand. Good old Ge Ge. Always finding opportunities to eat.

A few minutes later, Ivie came sprinting to the bus stop. She was panting, like she'd run the whole way. She was just in time. Right after she arrived, the bus pulled up and we had to get on or Mr. Stevie would yell at us.

A few days later, Olivia, Ivie, and I were standing in the same spot, trembling with anticipation. We were too scared to talk. It was the day of the castings. On the bus, we sat, still as statues. A few times Ge Ge said stuff to me, but I couldn't respond. I was too nervous.

"Luolan," Olivia breathed. "My head feels hot."

"That's because Connor Bakey's breathing on it," I whispered back.

"Connor," Ivie snapped. "Stop breathing on Olivia! Eavesdropper!"

Connor rolled his eyes and sat down.

Ivie shook her head. "Connor loves eavesdropping," she told me. "Such a weirdo."

That was the only conversation we had on the way to school.

* * *

"Gosh," Ivie cried, jumping up and down. "I am soooo scared!"

"Me too." I hugged her. "In case we don't all make it, break a leg!"

Just then, Mr. Caleb came in. Olivia squeezed my hand. Mr. Caleb pinned the casting list on the bulletin board. Olivia crushed my hand. Mr. Caleb left. Olivia let go of my hand and we swarmed toward the front of the room, determined to be the first to catch a glimpse of the paper. It was a long list, but my eyes jumped directly to the bottom.

Seaweed .... Luolan Xia

Seaweed. I. Am. A. Piece. Of. Seaweed. What?? How is this happening?!?! I stared at the cast list like it was a bomb about to explode. Then it dawned on me. Ms. Leonard. She was responsible for this. I needed to see Mr. Caleb.

"Luolan--" Olivia started. I pushed past her and into Mr. Caleb's office.

"Mr. Caleb?" I said. He raised his head from a pile of papers.

"Luolan? How can I help you?"

"I think there has been mistake."

Mr. Caleb frowned. "A mistake?"

"Or casting list is wrong." I gripped my backpack tighter. "It says on here I'm a piece of seaweed, but that's not even a part! I auditioned for Ursula, not piece of seaweed."

"Really?" Mr. Caleb rubbed his chin. "Ms. Leonard seemed to think that your audition was . . . how do I put it? Not for the sensitive ears."

I frowned. "What? No! Can audition for you right now!" With that, I began to sing 'Poor Unfortunate Souls'.

Mr. Caleb listened to my "audition" closely and thoughtfully. When I finished, he hesitated for a long time. Finally, he spoke.

"I do believe that you are qualified to be Ursula, Miss Luolan Xia," he announced in his quiet way. "I'll talk to the other performance teachers and we'll see what we can do. I'll report back to you tomorrow during class, okay?"

I nodded. "Okay." It was the best deal I could get. For now. "Thank you."

"You're welcome."

I sighed as I walked out of the room. Now all I could do was wait. Ugh.

"Ge Ge?" I asked my big brother that night. "Are you awake?"

"No."

I grinned. He totally was awake. "I need to tell you something."

"Ugh."

"Are you listening?"

"Maybe."

"You know how the cast list came out today?"

"Mmph."

"Well, I got the seaweed."

"What?"

"I got the seaweed," I repeated.

"Didn't you want Ursula?"

"Uh huh."

"Who got Ursula, then?"

"Berecca Arlard."

"The Banana girl?"

"Yeah. And her audition wasn't even that good!"

"That's unfair."

"I talked to Mr. Caleb, though."

"What did he say?"

"He said he would talk to the other performance teachers, then report back to me tomorrow."

"At least he's asking them."

"I guess. G'night, Ge Ge."

"Umph."

I started to turn off my light, but then I remembered one thing. I reached into my drawer and pulled out my list. 1. Make three new friends. Check. 2. Learn English. Check. 3. Get people to like me. Check. 4. Find a reason to call America 'home'. My eyes lingered on this one. I supposed that America felt more like my home now than it did a few weeks ago. But along with the good things that happened in America, bad things happened, too. I got into a fight with Haiqing. I got teased by Rennie and Cat. I was unfairly treated by Ms. Leonard.

I sighed and put the list back in my drawer. Nothing was this complicated back in China. At least not that I could remember. My biggest worries had been Yuan Lao Shi's English pop quizzes, how to retort to Dongqiang Zhang's annoying comments, and how to convince Mama to get me the newest fruit snacks at the market. How I wished to have worries as simple as those again.

I missed Haiqing so much. She was probably content right now, playing with Ziwei and going to her house for lunch. Just like she used to do with me. She probably didn't miss me at all.

I glanced at the balloon floating beside my bed. The one that Chance gave me for free. 'Never stop facing your fears. Always take chances.' If only it were as easy as it seemed.

Dinner with the Enemy

"Can someone please tell the class about the Great Depression?" Mrs. Bradley, our history teacher asked. "Luolan?"

I jumped, startled. I hadn't been paying attention. "Sorry?"

"The Great Depression."

"Uh, the Great Depression was…" I desperately grasped for the information I read in my history book last night. "It was a depression." *Wow. Way to go, Luolan.* "And it was very, very bad. A lot of people lost jobs."

"Yes," Mrs. Bradley sighed, as if she hoped for me to get it wrong. "Correct. My grandfather was in the depression, in fact…"

Whatever she said after that, I didn't hear her. I was too busy worrying about theater class. What would Mr. Caleb's decision be? Would I get the part?

Finally, the bell rang. Kids streamed into the halls. Our second-period history class joined them, Mrs. Bradley calling after us, "Your homework is to read the chapter on President Franklin Delano Roosevelt and answer the multiple choice questions!"

Ivie, Olivia and I hurried to Mr. Caleb's classroom. My heart was pounding. Would he say yes? Would I get my role? Or would I get stuck being a useless piece of seaweed forever?

We sat down at desks in the front of the room. A moment later, Mr. Caleb approached, going to the blackboard and writing something on it: *Little Mermaid* preparations.

"Okay, class," Mr. Caleb said. "Today is our first rehearsal of *The Little Mermaid*. Please form a circle around the keyboard. Luolan, Berecca, a word?"

Olivia squeezed my hand and off I went. Mr. Caleb greeted us at his desk. "Good day, girls. Luolan, I'm sure you know what this is about?"

I nodded.

"Great," Mr. Caleb clasped his hands together. "So, Berecca. The other performance teachers and I have come to the decision that seaweed is not the best role for Luolan. So, as she was originally auditioning for Ursula, you and Luolan will split the role, with you, Berecca, being Ursula in Act I, and you, Luolan, being Ursula in Act II."

My brain could not register the words. Me. Split with the Banana girl. *WHAT?!?!?!?!?!?!?!*

I could tell Berecca was feeling the same shock because her mouth was open like a codfish, and she was staring at me like I had grown another eye. Apparently, Mr. Caleb didn't notice because he clapped his hands like everything was okay.

"Awesome. So! Berecca, Luolan, go join the cast at the keyboard. I'm going to speak with the crew for a minute and then I'll be there." He grinned at us. "And thanks for being flexible!"

Flexible indeed. I sighed. This was NOT what I had expected. Nevertheless, I walked over and joined the cast of *The Little Mermaid* in front of the keyboard.

* * *

"Ow! You just bumped into me!"

I groaned for the millionth time. Berecca knew perfectly well I hadn't bumped into her--she fell on one of the fake rocks. I scooted back a few steps and kept on dancing.

"And twirl and bounce and--no, Ethan. You look like a kangaroo! Don't bounce so high." Mr. Caleb pretended to shake his finger at him.

Ethan looked embarrassed. He turned and looked at me as if he expected me to judge him. I gave him a reassuring smile.

"Let's take it from the top! And one, two, three, four!" Mr. Caleb started the soundtrack for 'Under the Sea'. "And swish, two, three, four. Step, two, three, four. Grapevine. Turn everyone, let's go. And bounce. No, not like a kangaroo, Ethan. That's better. Back row up, front row up, bridge. You two, go! Pay attention!"

At his command, Ivie and Veronica tiptoed offstage.

"And swish, step, glide," Mr. Caleb continued, issuing orders like a general. "Change lines. Change lines again. *I want more facial expression.* Front line, why are you facing the wrong way? Come on, everyone, get your feet off the ground. Ben, *why are you still on stage?*" The music stopped. The dance was done. Mr. Caleb took a big drink from his water bottle.

"Good job, everyone. Take a break. Get a drink. Next, we're going to run the scene between Ariel, Flounder, Sebastian and King Triton."

Olivia and Ivie came up to me. "Whew!" Ivie exclaimed, fanning her face. "I am soooo hot!"

I laughed. "Mr. Caleb is pretty intense, huh?"

Olivia grinned. "Yeah! Let's go get a drink."

When we got back from the water fountain, Mr. Caleb was organizing everyone into groups. Ivie and Olivia were in the same group, but I wasn't. In my group were Ethan, Ellie Azalea, Berecca, Curtis O'Connor, Hayley Dellan, and Abby Fergus-Falls.

"Your group will go over the music together," Mr. Caleb told us. "Anyone who is off-book, feel free to do it without your script." He left, and our group faced each other.

"Sooooo," Abby started, trying to make small talk. I didn't know much about her, but I knew she was on the school soccer team, she wore contacts, and she was very energetic. Today, Abby's honey-colored hair was pulled into a loose bun and she wore a 'Save the Whales!' t-shirt. "How was everyone's day?"

"The day has barely started," Berecca replied snarkily, flipping her dark brown hair over her shoulder. "So how should we know?"

Hayley frowned at her. "That's not very nice. Abby was just trying to start the conversation." Hayley's hair was strawberry blonde with streaks of purple and blue in it. She wore green framed glasses and had dark blue braces.

Berecca rolled her eyes at Hayley but stayed silent. Ellie cleared her throat. "Um, okay. So which song should we do first?"

I remembered that Ellie had been one of the ones laughing at me when I stood up in homeroom on the first day of school. She seemed okay now. At least, not about to start making fun of me.

"Maybe that first song, 'Daughters of Triton?'" Hayley suggested.

Berecca made a face. "You're the only mersister here."

"Berecca, stop making snide comments at every little thing we say," Ethan told her. Berecca sighed and sat down.

"I can sing the other parts for you," Abby told her.

"I can help," Ellie added.

"Me too," I said.

"I can sing Flounder," Curtis volunteered.

Ethan smiled at Berecca, an *I told you so* smile. Berecca rolled her eyes. We all ignored her. Hayley counted us off and we sang.

That afternoon, I rode the bus home with Ge Ge, Ivie, and Olivia after a successful theater practice. My mood was cheerful, despite Berecca's snarky behavior during class.

"Hey guys," Olivia said. We turned to look at her. "Don't you think that Berecca is just a bit mean?"

"A bit?" Ivie joked.

"Yeah," I replied. "I think bananas are supposed be soft and mushy and sweet! Berecca prickly as durian fruit!"

We all laughed. Then it was our stop and we had to get off, so Mr. Stevie wouldn't yell at us.

I entered my house and a smell hit my nose that I immediately recognized. "Dumplings!" I cried and ran into the kitchen.

Sure enough, Mama was making dumplings. Ming Ming sat in his high chair, singing a song about mud and making his toy dinosaurs butt heads.

"Hello, Luolan," Mama addressed me in Chinese. "How was your day?"

"Fine. Mama, why are you making dumplings?"

Mama winked. "It's a surprise."

Ming Ming squealed. He loved surprises.

"Lizhong!" Mama called to Ge Ge. "Come down and help me with the fish!"

"Fish?" I asked in disbelief. "Mama, why are you doing all this cooking?"

"Because we have an important guest coming and I want to make sure everything is perfect for her."

"*Shui?*" It definitely could not be Olivia or Ivie because they would most certainly tell me.

"I heard from her mother that she knows some Mandarin, too!" Then it hit me, <u>boom</u>! *Rennie* was the important guest coming over! What? How did Mama even know Rennie? Did she know that Rennie made fun of Ge Ge and me at the mall?

"Luolan? Are you okay?"

"Um . . . yeah. I'm fine."

"Okay. In that case, would you mind helping me set up the durian cakes?"

I nodded, making my way over to the cabinet and taking out the plates. I busied myself filling the plates with crispy treats so I wouldn't have to look at Mama's excited face. Rennie was coming. What was I going to do?

I checked to make sure Mama wasn't looking, then swiped a piece of Ming Ming's Halloween candy from the bin. It calmed me down a bit.

Ge Ge, Mama, and I worked side by side for an entire hour cooking, cleaning, and setting the table. At one point, Baba came to help us, but then he started getting a bunch of phone calls from his office, so he had to get back to work.

Finally, when the clock hit 5:30, the doorbell rang. I held my breath. Ge Ge and I looked at each other. I whispered who it was to him while we were chopping potatoes and he was just as horrified as I was.

"Rennie," I mouthed. He made a terrified face.

"*Bonjour!*" a familiar voice sang. "*Konnichiwa!*" I closed my eyes wearily. A Mandarin speaker indeed! If she spoke Mandarin, then I was a llama.

Rennie, her mom, a man I assumed was her father, and an unfamiliar girl all stepped into our house.

Somehow, Mama managed to smile. "Welcome, Rennie. This is Anya?" Mama hadn't had much time to learn English, so she was still a bit shaky with it.

"Hi, I'm Ann," said a girl from behind Rennie, waving. She stepped forward. She had the same straight brown hair and blue eyes as Rennie. She wore frameless glasses and a serious expression. She looked to be about fourth or fifth grade.

"Ann," Mama corrected. "Welcome our home."

"Yeah, yeah." Rennie walked past her and tromped into the kitchen. Still wearing her shoes.

"Rennie!" Ann paused to take off her shoes, then ran over to her sister. "Rennie! You're s'posed to take your shoes off!"

Rennie sniffed. "Huh."

"Mom," Ann looked at her mother pleadingly. I had a feeling this often happened in the Ball household.

"Renalda, darling," Mrs. Ball drawled. "Make our hosts happy and take off your shoes, precious."

Precious? Rennie was definitely anything but that.

Mr. Ball shifted uncomfortably. "Rennie, take off your shoes," he commanded. Rennie looked up at him with puppy-dog eyes. He frowned at her. "Now."

I sighed. Ann looked at me apologetically as if to say, *I know, right? I feel your pain.* I returned her look with a smile, then tried to smother my giggles as Ming Ming blew a raspberry at Rennie.

"Now we eat," Baba declared, breaking the uncomfortable silence. Mr. and Mrs. Ball took off their shoes and followed him to the dining room, Ann trailing behind. Mr. Ball turned a sharp gaze on Rennie as he left. Rennie rolled her eyes and reluctantly kicked her shoes off. They landed in a heap next to the staircase. Mama pursed her lips but stayed silent. Ge Ge and I exchanged frustrated glances. Finally, we turned and followed Rennie and the others into the dining room.

"Wow! This dinner is so exotic!"

I rolled my eyes so hard that the whites showed. This was the second snarky comment that Rennie had made over dinner. The first occurred when Rennie entered the dining room. She got a glimpse of the fish and said, "Ew! That fish has eyes! So not eating that!"

"Exotic?" Baba frowned. "What is the meaning?"

No one answered. Ann was busy glaring daggers at Rennie. Mr. Ball looked torn between his hosts and his daughter. Mrs. Ball was enjoying her food, blissfully ignoring the silence. Ge Ge and I didn't want to complicate things by answering the question. Ming Ming and Mama didn't know the meaning either, so they couldn't help.

Baba looked at the rest of us, a question in his eyes. Then he turned his attention back to his plate of fish. Perfectly good fish. Fish that Ge Ge and I took half an hour to prepare. Fish that annoying Rennie was staring at like it was poison. She was such a brat.

"Ugh," Rennie whined. "Ew. This Chinese food is so weird. Hey, Daddy? Do I honestly have to eat all this stuff?" Rennie was really pushing it. If she said one more word about the food then I would probably feel the need to punch her.

"Ahem." Mr. Ball cleared his throat. "Renalda?" Mr. Ball's tone was deadly quiet. I noticed that he called Rennie by her full name. Usually, getting called by your full name meant you did something wrong.

"Why, Daddy?" Rennie was obviously in trouble, couldn't she tell? Perhaps she never had anyone mad at her in her life. She always had her way.

Mr. Ball looked apologetically at Mama and Baba. He looked at Mrs. Ball, as if asking her what she wanted to do, but she was still eating. He stood up and pushed in his chair.

"Rennie. Come with me." Mr. Ball was being pretty clear now that Rennie was in trouble.

She sighed. "Okay, fine!"

Rennie followed her father out of the room. Ann, who sat between me and Ge Ge, leaned over and whispered, "I'm really sorry. Our parents--well, Mom, mostly, have been spoiling her since the day she was born. She *always* gets her way. Pizza for dinner, expensive belts for Christmas that she never even wears, you name it. Whatever she wants, she gets."

I laughed softly, deciding then and there that I liked Ann.

"Hey, Ann," I told her, "Want go get more *tang hulu* in the kitchen?" Ann nodded, playing along.

"Sure!"

We got out of our seats and walked to the kitchen.

"We haven't officially met yet," Ann pointed out once we were there. She held out her hand. "Hi. I'm Anya Irene Ball, but I go by Ann. I'm in fifth grade at Longwell Elementary. My older sister Rennie is a spoiled brat and got even more spoiled about a year ago, but I got used to her. Nice to meet you."

I giggled at her reference to Rennie. I held my hand out. "You too, Ann. My name is Luolan Xia. I am in sixth grade at Andrew Jackson Middle School. I have an older brother named Lizhong, but I call him Ge Ge. He's not annoying. I also have younger brother named Ming Ming. He is not annoying either. Most of time. Shall we be friends?"

"Of course, Luolan."

"Glad to hear, Ann." I started walking back to the dining room, but Ann stopped me.

"We were s'posed to be getting *tang hulu*, right?" she asked me. "Wouldn't it look suspicious if we came back empty-handed?"

"Yeah," I agreed. We each picked up some of the sweet red treats. Ann took a bite of one. Her eyes widened with delight.

"These are *so good!*" she exclaimed. "I'm totally asking for these for my eleventh birthday!"

"You can take extra when you leave. You share with Rennie," I teased.

Ann grinned. "Yeah. I'll share it with her. I'll share it with her alright, I'll put it in her hair and watch her try to comb it out." She grinned evilly. "Rennie's nuts about her hair."

I laughed as we walked back to the dining room. Maybe dinner with the enemy wouldn't be so bad after all.

Too Many Poems

"Guys, we need to focus," Skylar pleaded. "The exhibition is next week! We have to get our projects done!"

I groaned. It wasn't fair. Ethan and I were already done with our project; a poem about moving to America. It wasn't our fault everyone else wasn't.

Stop it! I told myself. *You're starting to sound like Rennie. It's just that other people work a bit slower, that's all!* I took a breath and put the finishing touches on my poem. It read:

LEAVING
a poem by
Luolan Xia and Ethan Arnold

Packing my bags
Dunno what to bring
Good-byes all around
Boarding the plane
Teasing my brother
A gift from my friend

Leaving China
to start again
"Flight number 23!"
Oh that's my cue
Good-bye
good-bye
I'll never forget you

I studied it with satisfaction. Perfect. Ethan leaned over my shoulder and stared at it.

"It's missing something, don't you think?" he asked.

I furrowed my eyebrows. "No. What?"

"I'm not sure. It just seems . . . kind of ordinary. It's not unique."

Ben Feindale, the guy who played Flotsam in *The Little Mermaid* leaned over my shoulder to study it. "I'll say!" he exclaimed after a while. "Looks exactly like Jamie's and mine!"

I frowned at him. "What do you mean?"

Ben showed us his poem. "See?" he asked. "Exactly the same. Except for the words, of course. Mine is much shorter than yours. Well, it's based on Jamie's grandma. But Jamie's not here today, so I'll just call it mine."

I read it over. It said:

IMMIGRANTS

by Ben Feindale and Jamie Quinton

My great-grandma immigrated
to the U.S.
in 1921
She immigrated
to the Land of Opportunity,
found a better life,
and became a proud American

"Great!" I smiled politely. "That was really good."

"Did you see what Lilah and Angela are making?" Ben gushed. "Soooo good!"

I held back a laugh. Everyone knew Ben had a crush on Lilah Rodriguez.

"What are they making?" Ethan asked, pointedly changing the subject.

"A poem."

"*Another poem?*" I felt so frustrated. Why was everyone writing poems?

Ethan must have guessed my thoughts because he called over to the other tables, "Hey, CJ! What are you and Curtis making?"

CJ Moines and Curtis O'Connor both looked up at the sound of Ethan's voice. "A poem," CJ answered. "Wanna read it?"

"No thanks," Ethan replied, glancing at me. I nodded, motioning to Skylar. We walked up to her.

"Uh, Skylar?" I asked.

She glanced at me. "Hey Luolan. What's up?"

"Everyone's writing poems."

"What do you mean?"

"Exactly what it sounds like," Ethan jumped in. "Everyone's writing poems. Luolan and I wrote a poem, Kira and Carolyn wrote a poem, Ben and Jamie wrote a poem, you name it!"

Skylar looked worried. "But there's supposed to be writing from all different genres!"

We nodded. "Yeah. But apparently, no one is taking that into consideration," Ethan said with a small smile.

"What should we do?" I asked.

"Well, maybe we could turn it into a poetry festival," Skylar tried.

"Yeah . . . no." Ethan shook his head. "No offense, Skylar, but that's sort of a lame idea. Also, we're the writing club! We can do something better."

Skylar sighed. "I know."

"What are we going to do?" I asked desperately. "We can't have everyone write poems!"

Skylar smacked her head with the palm of her hand, as if to loosen up her thinking muscles. "I'll think of something," she muttered, wincing and rubbing her head. "Don't worry. I'll think of something." She hesitated. "Or not."

Ethan groaned. "Very reassuring, Skylar."

She sighed, absently checking her watch. Then she jumped up. "Guys, it's time to go," she called. We all scrambled, shoving our projects into our bags. I passed Rennie and Cat on the way out, but I didn't speak to them and they ignored me as well. They hadn't been in writing club when I first joined. I wondered why they decided to come

As I was walking out, my phone binged with a text. I knew it was from Ge Ge right away because it was written in Chinese;

Ge Ge: Meet me in the Cold Cold Ice Cream Shoppe after writing club! There with Ming Ming right now.

I grinned. An ice cream cone was exactly what I needed.

I got off at a bus stop that was close to the Cold Cold Ice Cream Shoppe. I spotted Ge Ge and Ming Ming waving at me as I came closer.

"Hey! Luolan!" Ming Ming was shouting at the top of his lungs in Chinese. "We got ice cream!"

"Shh," Ge Ge laughed. "Be quiet, you great howler monkey!"

Ming Ming bounced on his lap. "Ice cream ice cream howler monkey ice cream!"

I made a face. "Howler monkey ice cream? Sounds gross." I sat down at their table, and Ge Ge handed me a green tea cone, my favorite.

I thanked him and slurped a melting drop of sweet ice cream.

"Howler monkey!" Ming Ming squealed. "Luolan eat howler monkey!" I made a monkey face at him, and he erupted into giggles.

"What happened today?" Ge Ge asked me. I blinked.

"Huh?"

"You have a 'something happened today' look about you," he explained.

I rolled my eyes. "Oh, the usual: Cat and Rennie trying to copy my homework, Willa Masons dropping her lunch bag instead of her trash into the compost bin, Jack Lewitt and Jack Browning fighting about who has the better last name."

Ge Ge burst out laughing. "That's *the usual?* Then what's the unusual? Wait, don't tell me. I don't want to know."

I took a paper out of my bag and began to write. Ge Ge leaned over and stared at it. "How to Save the Writing Festival," he read. "What?"

I sighed. "The writing club festival. We're all supposed to write in different genres, but everyone's writing poems. I'm trying to think of an easy solution."

Ge Ge thought for a moment. "There is no easy solution."

I glared at him. "Very helpful."

"Luolan ice cream go bye bye," Ming Ming said sadly. I looked down at my ice cream and found that it had indeed melted all over my shirt.

"Ugh," I groaned. "Better go home and change."

"You go," Ge Ge replied. "I'll follow you with Ming Ming."

I nodded. Maybe I would see Chance again. I still had the yellow balloon he gave me for free.

As I stepped out of the shop, I saw two of my least favorite people, Rennie and Cat, with Ann trailing behind them. Rennie snickered at my ice cream-covered shirt.

"What happened, Ulan?" she asked snarkily. "Ice cream on your shirt? Like, yuck!"

"Rennie," Ann began, but Rennie cut her off.

"And what happened to your hair?" she continued. "You look like you've been rolling in mud!"

I knew it wasn't true, for I had just brushed my hair this morning. Still, I was tempted to run. *No*, I told myself. *Don't be a coward.* I studied Rennie, looking for something I could retort her on. My eyes landed on her long brown hair. It was pulled back into a fancy bun, with dozens of bobby pins and barrettes in it. I stifled a giggle, remembering what Ann had said about Rennie being nuts about her hair.

"You are one to talk," I found myself saying. I gestured at Rennie's hair, making a *you know what I'm talking about?* face. Cat giggled in spite of herself.

Rennie glared at me. "Say what, Ulan?"

"I am not scared of you, Rennie," I replied evenly. "So stop wasting your time on me and do something else. Ann here can give you some examples, right?"

Ann grinned and gave me a thumbs up. "On it, Luolan."

"You--you just..." Rennie turned on her heels and marched off, leaving Cat and Ann to scramble after her.

At the last moment, Ann turned her head and gave me a humongous *thank you* grin. I grinned back, feeling like a huge weight had been lifted off my shoulders.

When I got home, I took out my phone and checked my messages. There was a text from Ivie.

> Ivie: Hey Luolan, did you hear? We're doing email pals in Chinese class! It's like pen pals but with emails.

I responded right away:

Luolan: Rlly? Who told you?

Ivie: Mrs. Babbity, the Languages Head. She told me in study hall

Luolan: Wow. With who?

Ivie: We're sposed 2 pick random names from a bag or something

Luolan: RANDOM? If I end up with some1 that used kno?

Ivie: LOL. That would b sooo hilarious. U could be like "Hey this is Luolan I'm writing from my new school, how's life in China?"

Luolan: Haha :) Wut if it's Dongqiang Zhang?

Ivie: Who's that

Luolan: An annoying boy from China

Ivie: Ooh! That would be soooooooo weird

Luolan: Yea

Ivie: Gtg do homework

Luolan: Ok. Bye

In spite of what Ivie said, I still worried. What if I got someone I used to know? It would be so awkward and it might make me feel homesick.

I set the worry aside and took out my homework. Eleven times ten equals one hundred ten. A sense of familiarity washed over me. I had done this problem when I took that easy math test on the last day of school back in China.

A feeling of sadness and longing washed over me. Why did we choose to move to America? Why was Haiqing mad at me? I remembered Jamie's and Ben's poem we read today. Jamie's great-grandmother may have found a better life here in America, but would I?

My Email Pal

Two days later, I was in the theater room, warming up my voice. We were going to learn the choreography for *Poor Unfortunate Souls* and I wanted to come during study hall to warm up. Just then, the "class-is-starting-in-five-minutes" bell rang and kids started swarming the halls. I spotted Olivia and ran to catch up with her.

"Email pals!" Olivia squealed as soon as she saw me.

I stifled a groan. "Yay."

"What's wrong?" she asked.

"Afraid I'll get someone used to know," I explained.

Olivia nodded. "That must be stressful."

"It is. Know what school we email to?"

She shook her head.

We walked into the classroom. Olivia and I sat at desks across from each other. Ivie tapped my shoulder and waved me over. She looked unhappy.

"What's wrong?" I asked.

"My parents split up," she explained. "My dad moved away this morning."

"Oh!" Olivia and I exclaimed at the same time.

"I'm so sorry, Ivie!" I cried, while Olivia patted her on the back.

"It's okay. I'm actually not that sad about it," Ivie said.

"*What*?!" we exclaimed so loudly that a few people turned to look at us.

"Well, I am sad that my dad is moving away, of course," Ivie explained, "but I'll still get to visit him on weekends and during vacations. I know things will never really be the same ever again, but we're all getting a fresh start and that's what I'm grateful for."

"Wow." Olivia stared at her in awe. "I'd be devastated if my family split up. I'd lock myself in my room and never come out."

I nodded, agreeing completely. I couldn't imagine a life without Mama or Baba.

Ivie laughed. "I am sad, but it's gonna make both my mom and dad happier and that's what counts. Besides, both my mom and dad found really great jobs and we'll probably get to move out of the campsite!" She did a little happy dance in her seat. "We still won't get our own car though. But still. You see? I'll get used to it. We all will."

Olivia and I stared at her, in awe of her maturity. A few minutes later, Mrs. Henford, our teacher, walked in. She wasn't Chinese, but she actually spoke the language pretty well. She was also my advisor, a teacher I could go to if I "needed to talk".

"Alright, class!" Mrs. Henford called in her high, squeaky voice. We were supposed to quiet down, but no one did except for me, Olivia, and Ivie.

"*Shut it!*" Olivia hollered. Everyone stared at her, surprised, but they quieted down.

"Ahem!" Mrs. Henford cleared her throat. "Thank you," she said to Olivia. "*Anyway*, class, we're going to be doing a very special project for the next two months." She struck a dramatic pose. Everyone looked bored. Mrs. Henford looked at us expectantly.

"Yay?" Ivie tried. Mrs. Henford sighed.

"*Anyway,*" she said pointedly.

"Is that her favorite word or something?" Olivia whispered to me. I giggled in spite of myself.

"Miss Xia, is what you and Miss Deacon talking about right now more relevant than my class?" she asked me, frowning.

"No, Mrs. Henford," I replied quickly, looking back at the blackboard, where Mrs. Henford had written 'Email Pals'.

A kid sitting in the back waved his hand in the air. I remembered his name: Donny, and that he was in my history class and made fun of me during my first week, but I didn't remember anything else about him. Before Mrs. Henford said his name, Donny started speaking.

"Uh...I think you wrote that wrong, Mrs. Henford. It's pen pals." Donny said bluntly.

"Don't call out, Mr. O'Sullivan. I am not wrong. We are calling it email pals because instead of using letters, we are using the internet. We are doing this project with a school in China. Our school is picking the names of our email pal and sending the first email. Your email pal does not know who you are. Whoever you get now will be your email pal for the rest of the unit. No trading, no objecting. Now! Would everyone please get out their iPads?"

I raised my hand. "Yes, Luolan?"

"Mrs. Henford, you can't access gmail in China," I told her.

She sighed in exasperation. "The kids in China can access gmail once in a while to see their emails from you and send emails back. Now, go get your iPads!"

Everyone scrambled to get their iPads out. I looked around. Most of the other iPads had various sauces and crumbs on them, but mine didn't. I always kept my iPad in my backpack when I wasn't using it. Not that Mrs. Henford noticed. Odd, considering that the iPads cost over six hundred dollars. All she cared about was if kids were talking in class or if they called out without raising their hands.

"Sign into your iPads," Mrs. Henford instructed. We all did, then she told us to click the 'mail' button. I clicked mine, clicked the "new mail" and a fresh blank document popped up.

Mrs. Henford cleared her throat. She took out a Yankees baseball cap from her desk drawer. "When I call your name, please come up and pick a name from this hat," she told us. "Lars Abramson."

One by one, she called our names. I watched as Ivie picked a name, smiled, then sat down. The same reaction came from Olivia. Rennie (who by some bad luck also took Chinese) just read her name and sighed.

Finally, it was my turn. I took a deep breath and stood up. I picked a name. It was a girl named Zhou Mei. At least it wasn't anyone I knew.

"Okay, class!" Mrs. Henford said as I walked back to my seat. "Your first one-paragraph email pal assignment is due tomorrow. Check it with me before you mail it, though."

We all nodded, packed up our iPads, and put them in our bags. Then we all pushed and shoved to be the first one out of the door.

"So, who'd you get?" Ivie asked as we squeezed out of the overcrowded doorway. "Someone you used to know?" she teased.

"Ha." I punched her lightly in the shoulder. "Who'd you get?"

She shrugged. "This boy—Wu something something. I forgot his name."

"Well you better remember before you send your first email," I told her.

She laughed. "C'mon. Let's go see who Olivia got."

That night, I typed up an email to Zhou Mei. I asked her about her school, her teachers, and her hobbies. Then I closed my iPad and carefully stashed it back into my backpack. Just then, Ming Ming waddled into my room.

"Luolan?" he whispered. "I'm scared. My room full of shadow monsters."

I giggled. "Aww. Come on in, Ming Ming. You can sleep in my bed."

Ming Ming snuggled into my bed as I brushed my teeth and changed. Then I got into bed with Ming Ming and pulled the covers over our heads.

"Good nighty night, Luolan!" Ming Ming sang.

"Shhh," I shushed him. "People are sleeping! Good night, Ming Ming."

I closed my eyes, wishing my problems were as simple as Ming Ming's and his imaginary shadow monsters. I thought I would never fall asleep. I was wrong. In less than five minutes, I was in the land of dreams.

Tough Times

"**C**ome *on*, Luolan!" Ge Ge complained. "We'll miss the *xiao che! The bus!*"

"Coming!"

I dashed out the door with Ge Ge at my heels yelling for me to wait up. I arrived just in time to see the bus pull up in front of the stop. We hopped on, along with Ivie and Olivia.

"I can't wait for Chinese class!" Ivie sang. "We get to send our emails!"

"Ugh," a voice said from behind us. "You're *excited* for *that?*"

I sighed. Rennie.

Ivie turned and raised an eyebrow. "You're not?"

"I don't like my partner," muttered Rennie. "She's sooo boring."

Olivia rolled her eyes. "You haven't even met her yet, Rennie," she said. "How do you know she's boring?"

"Her name sounds boring," Rennie replied.

"And what's her name?" I asked.

"Li Wen, *Ulan.*"

I frowned, but not because of the way she pronounced my name. Why did that name sound so familiar? Then I got it. Li Wen was a girl Haiqing and I used the play with, before she moved to a new neighborhood.

"Uh, Luolan?" Olivia asked. "You okay?"

I blinked. "Yeah. Yeah, I'm fine."

"Well then let's get on the bus." I looked up and saw that, sure enough, the big yellow bus had pulled up without me noticing.

"Okay," I said, pushing my thoughts out of my head. I'd deal with them later.

As the bus pulled into the school curb, I quadruple-checked my backpack to make sure I had my iPad. I did. Good. I didn't want today— the day we were starting our email pal project—to be the day that I forgot my homework.

"Luolan! You coming?" Olivia called. I nodded and ran to catch up with them.

Our first period was math. I half zoned out, for I already knew all the math they were teaching anyway.

"Divide the decimal by three . . . blah blah blah . . . test tomorrow . . . yakkity yakkity yak . . . pass those down please, Miss Kelly, pay attention...drone drone drone . . . here's your homework..." our math teacher, Mr. González, droned on. Wait! He was talking about homework! It must be time to go!

I checked the clock. One minute! I held my breath.

"Have a nice day!"

Yes! I snatched my books from my desk and rushed out the door, hollering apologies to the kids I bumped into. I ran straight to my locker to put my math books away and get my iPad out. Then, I dashed to the Chinese classroom, signing into the device as I went.

"Luolan!" Ivie and Olivia were yelling. "Hold up! Wait for us!"

I slowed in front of the classroom, catching my breath. Ivie caught up with me a moment later, Olivia on her tail.

"Excited for Chinese, aren't ya?" Ivie asked, grinning.

I nodded, my face flushed from running. "Yeah."

We sat down at the front of the room.

"Good morning, class," Mrs. Henford announced a few minutes later. She sat down behind her desk and eyeing a few latecomers suspiciously as they tried to slip in without her noticing. They lowered their heads and avoided her eyes.

"As you know, we will be sending our first email pal emails today," Mrs. Henford began. She went on to tell us about more things that we would be doing with our email pals. I tapped my foot impatiently. I was really looking forward to start the project.

"Please line up in front of my desk for me to check your emails," Mrs. Henford finally instructed. "In alphabetical order, please."

We all rushed to the front of the room, lining up with me last. Ugh, I hated being last.

Mrs. Henford began checking emails.

Smile.

Nod.

"Good job."

"Go fix that."

"This is unacceptable!"

"Nice work."

Large smile.

Finally, it was my turn. I stepped up to Mrs. Henford's desk and gave her my iPad. She read over my work. Finally, she nodded.

"Good job, Luolan," she told me. "This is great."

I smiled at her. "Thanks, Mrs. Henford."

After I sat down, Mrs. Henford stood up. "You may send your emails." Finally!

I pressed send and closed my iPad.

That afternoon, I headed to writing club. I still had no plan for our project dilemma, but I figured I should go and help Skylar figure one out.

I opened the door and found her sitting in the middle of the room, trying to think while kids chattered all around her, and an eighth grade guy drew on the whiteboard. "Hi, Skylar," I said loudly.

"Oh, hi, Luolan," replied Skylar. "Got any ideas?"

I hadn't, but Ge Ge's words, "There is no easy solution," gave me inspiration.

"Maybe. Can you get everyone to quiet down?"

Skylar nodded. "_Hey!_" she yelled, hands cupped over her mouth. Everyone instantly fell silent. The guy drawing on the whiteboard tiptoed back to his seat

"I know you are all looking for an easy way to fix the project problem," I began, "But there's no easy way." Mutterings began and I raised my hand for silence. "We have to redo our projects."

"What?!" Ben complained. "But we worked so hard on our poem!"

"I know you did," I replied. "We're *all* remaking our projects." To my surprise, no one objected, in fact, they all seemed intrigued by the idea.

"That's a pretty good idea," Ethan acknowledged. He smiled at me. I blushed back.

"I want you all to write down what your project is going to be," I added, feeling more comfortable now that everyone agreed with me. "We don't want anymore . . . *complications*."

Skylar smiled at me. It was a grateful smile, the smile of one who had just had a lot of pressure lifted from her shoulders. She clasped her hands together. "Okay, you lot, you heard what Luolan said! Let's get to work, writing club!"

I grinned to myself. Despite all that had happened today, here I was now, as happy as a person could be. It was exhilarating!

* * *

As I sat on the couch that afternoon, doing homework, my phone lit up, signaling that I had mail. Who was it? I wondered. Ivie and Olivia usually texted, as far as I knew, no one else had my email.

I picked up my phone and turned on the screen. I almost jumped in surprise. It was Rennie! Why was *she* sending me an email?

I clicked on it and read:

YOU SAID YOU KNOW LUOLAN AND HER FRIEND, RIGHT?

Well of course I knew Luolan, I *was* Luolan. This was strange. Still, I read on.

AND YOU SAID THEY GOT INTO A FIGHT? WHAT FIGHT? WHAT HAPPENED? TELL ME, LI WEN, PLEASE? WHY DID THEY FIGHT?

I just sat there, shocked. So the email had been intended for Li Wen. Rennie just accidentally sent it to me. But Li Wen told Rennie about what happened at the camping trip? How did she even know what happened? Had Haiqing told her? That was probably logical, since Li Wen was also one of Haiqing's friends.

Still, I couldn't help feeling a little bit hurt. I'd been involved, too. I should have a say in what Haiqing says. Although, Haiqing *still* wasn't texting me, and I doubted she would want to ask me.

But why did Haiqing call it a fight? It hadn't been a full-out fight, just a disagreement. Then I remembered what I'd said, that I didn't care about being friends with her. Okay, maybe it was more of a fight than I thought.

I had one more question: why did Rennie send the email to me? Perhaps she just typed in the first letter of the email address, and my name popped up. That was weird. She should've checked the name to make sure it was the correct one.

"Luolan!" Baba called from the kitchen, "Dinner is ready!"

I closed my phone and stood up. I would keep this a secret—for now.

Rennie's Birthday Party

"Luolan!" Mama called upstairs. "*Ni you xin!* You have mail!"

I sat up. I never got mail! I tore down the stairs and found myself facing a bright blue envelope labeled in fancy old-fashioned cursive: Ulan Xia, 28 Woodbury Ln Winston, Massachusetts. Before I opened the envelope I knew who it was from, even without reading the return address: Rennie.

Sure enough, inside the envelope was a letter, written in the same handwriting:

You are invited to Renalda Elisabeth Ball's twelfth birthday party!

When:　*November 30th, 2.00–5.00 P.M.*

Where:　*Rennie's house, 12 Robin Ave., Winston, MA.*

What:　*Rennie's 12th birthday.*

Hope you can attend, Ulan!

I sat limply down, glaring at the envelope like it had somehow offended me. Why had Rennie invited *me* of all people? Maybe her mom actually thought I was her friend and had made her invite me. Who knew?

"What is it, Luolan?" Mama asked me, entering the room.

"Um..." Should I tell her? If I told her, then she would most certainly make me go. Mama has always been big on not refusing invitations. But I didn't want to lie to my mother. "It's a . . . birthday..."

"*Shui?* Who's birthday? Olivia?"

"No..."

"Ivie?"

"No."

"Who?"

"Uh . . . Rennie?"

It came out as a question. I hadn't meant for it to, but Mama didn't notice.

"Rennie?" she gasped. "The girl who came over for dinner? She's a darling, so sweet and polite--"

"Mama..." I said, gritting my teeth. "She's *not.*"

"What do you mean? I saw her with my very own eyes. She's wonderful."

"But you don't go to school with her."

Mama's face filled with concern. "Is everything okay, Luolan? Is she being mean to you?"

I wanted desperately to tell Mama everything. I wanted her to understand. But I couldn't. You see, Mama has always been very overprotective of me and my siblings. If I told her, then she would probably just go tell the superintendent and make things more complicated than they needed to get. So I shook my head and forced a smile onto my face.

"Everything's fine, Mama," I replied. "Everything's just fine."

Mama smiled, relieved. "So it's settled? You're going?"

For a moment, I was confused. "Going where?"

"Rennie's birthday party!" Mama exclaimed, surprised that I had forgotten so soon.

"Do I have to?"

"Luolan..."

I sighed. "Mama..."

"It's impolite to refuse invitations."

"I guess, but I really don't like Rennie."

Mama sat next to me on the bed. "Sometimes in life we have to do things that we don't want to do."

I processed the words for a moment. Then I asked the question I had been waiting to ask for a really long time. "Mama? Why did we move here?"

The question seemed to take her by surprise. "Well . . . for starters, you children needed a better education."

"You always say that."

"There was also the two-child policy."

I was confused. I'd never heard of the policy before. "What's that?"

"In China, you can only have two kids. When we had Ming Ming, we had to pay a fine."

"We did?" I hadn't known that. "So technically, we bought Ming Ming?"

She laughed. "No. He's still ours."

"But we paid the fine already. What does that have to do with leaving China?"

Mama hesitated, as if deciding what to say. "Well . . . in truth, your baba and I were hoping to have another child."

I gasped. "Really?!"

She nodded. "We were still deciding the best time to tell you kids," Mama explained. "Neither your Ge Ge nor Ming Ming knows yet."

"When are you going to tell them?"

"Sometime soon."

"Are you sure that you're going to have a baby?"

"No. But we'll find out in good time. Meanwhile, you still need to go to Rennie's party."

"Ugh."

Mama smiled, patted my shoulder, then stood up and exited the room.

I stared blankly at the door, deep in thought. Mama was going to have a baby. Well, maybe. But if she had the baby . . . would it be a girl or a boy? Could we play with her?

Then it occurred to me. The new baby--if Mama had a baby--would be the first member of our family to be born in America. Would that make him any different than if he was born in China? I hoped not!

Five days later, I stood on Rennie's front porch holding a wrapped gift in my hands and dreading what was to come. Inside that box was a necklace with a dragon charm on it. It had loops in it so you could put charms on it. Personally, I didn't think Rennie deserved it.

The door swung open. I almost jumped out of my shoes.

"Hi, Ulan!" Rennie's mother exclaimed. She wore a poofy red dress, as if she were going to a wedding instead of her daughter's birthday party. "Come in! Everyone's been expecting you!"

Everyone? I gulped. How many people were there, exactly?

I stepped inside the house and took off my shoes. "Um . . . where should I..." I gestured toward my present.

Mrs. Ball waved me off. "Just put it anywhere you want," she replied airily. "It doesn't matter. We'll find it eventually."

I frowned. That didn't sound like a good idea. Mrs. Ball didn't sound like the most organized person in the world. Then again, maybe she just didn't care.

I set the box down on the kitchen counter for it seemed like the first spot Rennie would look. Then I took a deep breath and walked into the living room.

Inside, it seemed as if a zoo had sprouted overnight. Twenty girls roamed around, texting on their cell phones and eating Cheetos. Rennie spotted me and waved me over.

"Ulan!" she exclaimed, as if she were actually happy to see me. "Look! I decorated the living room China themed! You'll feel right at home here!"

I looked around, horrified, noticing for the first time the decorations on the mantle, the couches, and the walls. *Fu* signs--Chinese symbols for good luck--hung sideways, lopsided paper lanterns sat flopped over on the floor. Fortune cookie fortunes littered the ground. I fled.

I spent the majority of the party in the bathroom. I didn't dare come out for fear of what the other girls might say to me. Rennie was purposely making a fool of me in front of all the other girls. Or maybe she actually thought she was doing the right thing. That was even worse.

"Luolan?" a voice called softly from outside the bathroom. Ann. I looked at my phone. It was 4:30. I had been in the bathroom for two-and-a-half hours.

"Yeah." I opened the door a crack and peeked outside, just to make sure. Sure enough, Ann stood there, a placid expression on her face, holding a fortune cookie.

"Hey," she said. "Want a cookie?"

I made a face. "Ugh, no."

She giggled. "Yeah, I thought so."

"What are they doing?"

"Playing Pin the Tail on the Donkey."

"So they have stopped the 'Chinese' thing?"

"No, they're still at it. Rennie's cake was fortune cookie shaped with green tea ice cream on top." She rolled her eyes. "What's the point, you know?"

"Oh, I know."

"Come on out. The party's no fun without you."

"I'm not going to the party."

Ann laughed. "Didn't say you had to. Come on. I wanna show you something."

She pulled me out of the bathroom and we dashed down the hall. At the front door, we tugged on our shoes and put on our coats. We were just about to go outside when someone skidded to a stop in front of us. Ellie Azalea, the girl from homeroom who had laughed at me on the first day.

"Hi, Ellie," I mustered enough courage to say. "What are you doing?"

"This party is torture!" she cried, panting. "And I am *not* staying a minute longer!"

"I am *so* with you," Ann replied, taking over the conversation. "Want to come with us?"

"Sure!" Ellie replied gratefully. "Anything to get out of the party!"

"Come on!" I beckoned for her to follow us. "Ann's showing me a--" I looked at her for details.

"A secret place," Ann confirmed. "Now get your shoes on and let's go!"

Ann led us outside and around the back. She motioned for us to be quiet, saying, "No one knows about this place. We absolutely *cannot* let Rennie find out."

We gave her the thumbs up to show that we got it. Ann marched on. Finally, we arrived at the edge of the woods. Ellie glanced around nervously.

"Are we going into the woods?" she asked, anxiety showing in her voice. "I have claustrophobia."

Ann shook her head. "No. We're going in *there*." She pointed to a space between two large rocks I hadn't noticed before.

"I'm not sure if that's much better," Ellie replied, edging away.

"Relax," Ann told her. "It's larger than it looks."

Ellie still looked uneasy. I jumped in. "Ellie, if you don't like it in there, then I'm sure Ann won't mind if you run away as fast as you can. But for now, I wanna see what's in there."

Ellie grinned at me, obviously more relaxed. She seemed alright so far. She twirled a strand of her long brown ponytail around her index finger, thinking. Finally, she nodded. "Okay. I'll do it."

We cheered and Ann led the way in. It turned out that Ann was right. The space was bigger than it looked. It was so wonderful that Ellie took one look around and said, "I'm staying here forever."

We all laughed. I felt the same way. The space between the rocks widened until the space was big enough for three girls to move around. There, Ann had spread a checkered red-and-white picnic blanket and placed some throw pillows to make it more comfy. Wildflowers that grew in bunches all around us gave off a sweet-smelling scent.

Ann sat down and passed out mint Oreos. As I bit into mine, I remembered my first Oreo in America, which I bought with my babysitting money from the Baker family. I wondered how they were doing.

"Cheers!" Ellie said, holding up her Oreo. We clinked ours against hers.

"What you use place for?" I asked Ann. She shrugged.

"Oh, a number of things," she replied. "Escaping from my older sister, doing my homework, being alone. I discovered the place when I was in first grade. Rennie was bullying me and . . . well . . . yeah."

Ellie nodded wisely. "Oh, I can so relate. My older brother, Andy, is *the worst*. He tries to pulverize me every chance he gets." She shuddered. "Thank goodness he's in college now."

Ann grinned at her. Then she turned to me. "Any sibling problems, Luolan?"

I shook my head. "None. I have an older brother, Lizhong, but we're almost the same age. I also have a younger brother--Ming Ming, but he just talks shadow monsters and plays with zombie dolls."

Ellie coughed. "That's a creepy little brother you have there."

We all laughed. Ann checked her watch. "Oh no!" she exclaimed. "It's 5:10! Rennie's gonna kill me when she finds out I'm missing the party!"

We all scrambled up, hitting our heads on the rock in the process. ("Ow! Ow! Ow!") Just before we emerged from Ann's secret hideout, a voice called, "Annnnn-nieeeeee! Where are you? Come ou-uut!"

Ann groaned. "I'm gonna die."

We began our long trek up to the house.

Saving the Play

"Hey, Luolan, can you find my sash?" Adalie Falfale, the girl who played Jetsam asked. "We're going on in five minutes!"

"Here!" I took the glow-in-the-dark sash from the prop table and helped Adalie put it on. "You look great!"

"Thanks. Break a leg!" Adalie took a deep breath, then walked away, softly singing under her breath.

"You too. Break a leg," I called softly after her, repeating the traditional theater term for 'good luck'.

It was the day of the show. We were actually performing *The Little Mermaid* on the big Andrew Jackson Middle School stage! **_Agghhhhh_**!!!!!!

I double-checked myself. Leotard, check. Fancy twirly poofy skirt-thing, check. Tentacles, check. Heavy crown that made me feel faint, check. Gloves, check. I took a deep breath. I was ready.

I made my way to the wings on stage left, sneaking peeks at what was going on on stage. Ivie was singing *Part of Your World*, her clear, sweet soprano voice carrying out over the audience like church bells. She sounded wonderful.

When Ivie finished, the auditorium roared with applause. I could hardly keep myself from jumping up and down and cheering, even though Ivie and I were technically still fighting.

"Come on, Luolan," Adalie whispered to me. She and Ben were back from saying their lines on stage. "We're on soon. Then it's time for our song."

I gave them the double thumbs up. "I know. Thanks anyway."

"Anytime." Adalie turned and crept away with Ben, her glow-in-the-dark electric eel headdress bobbing around behind her.

Jacquelyn Meddleson, the stage manager, patted me on the back. She had a flashlight and shined it on the script. "Break a leg," she whispered.

I smiled at her, too nervous to speak. I watched Ivie say her lines, then Adalie and Ben crept onstage to say theirs. My brain didn't register anything.

Finally, Jacquelyn gave me a push. Then I was onstage.

It took me a moment for my brain to make sense of what was going on. Then instinct kicked in and I heard Ben say his line. I opened my mouth and began to speak.

Everything was going well until the middle of the song. I know, *extremely* bad timing. But it happened.

We were at a pause in the song where Ivie and I had a conversation with each other. I had just said my line and Ivie was supposed to say hers. From the look on her face, she forgot the line.

"But--" Ivie faltered. "But if I grow legs then I--"

The line was supposed to be, "But if you make me into a human, then how will I be with my friends and family again?" But Ivie had forgotten it completely.

The pause felt like forever. I awkwardly glanced at the audience and saw most of them looked worried. I knew I had to do something, but what?

"Whatever it is that you're worried about, I don't care," I proclaimed, improvising on the spot. "Now, do you want to become a human or not? Ten, nine, eight, seven, six--"

"Okay! Okay. I'll do it," Ivie interrupted, just as she was supposed to. Behind her, Adalie and Ben looked relieved. The play continued without a hitch.

Later, while I was backstage, taking my tentacles off, Ivie approached me.

"Hey, Luolan? Thanks," she said. "I shouldn't have forgotten my line, and I really do appreciate you saving me out there." She gestured at the stage. "So, thanks."

"You're welcome," I replied. "And it's okay. Everyone forgets their lines once in a while."

Ivie smiled. "I guess you're right. See you."

I waved and turned to put my costume away.

I met my parents in the lobby, Ming Ming beaming and holding out a bouquet of flowers.

"Good job," Ge Ge told me. "Nice save out there."

"You mean, you noticed?" I asked, my hopes deflating. The whole point of that save was to make sure people *didn't* notice.

Ge Ge shook his head. "Nah. Olivia told me just now."

"Bye, Luolan," Ivie said to me as she and her family passed by. They were getting a ride from Ellie Azalea's family since they didn't have a car. I noticed her dad was with them, looking a little awkward, but still there nonetheless.

"Bye," I told her, waving to Ellie at the same time I said the words. She waved back.

"Come on, Luolan, let's go!" Ming Ming squealed. "Let go let go let gooooooooo!"

"Okay, Ming Ming." I walked over and took a bouquet of flowers he handed me. "Thanks."

"Great job, Luolan," Baba said to me. He patted me on the back. "*Hao bang ya!* You were wonderful!"

"Thanks, Baba."

I felt as if my whole body had been encased in a warm shell that night, as people congratulated and complimented me. Nothing could harm me then, not a single mean word or action. It was as if I were walking on clouds.

Confessions

We had our first snow on Sunday. It was perfect. Back in Shanghai, China, we never really had more than one inch of snow. On Monday, we woke up to almost a foot of powdery cold goodness.

Ge Ge and I got up early to play in it. I joked to Ge Ge that he was too old to play anymore.

"Who cares?!" he cried, tossing a fistful of snow into the air. "Today, I'm ten-years-old again."

Ge Ge and I built a humongous snowman. He had a carrot nose, button eyes, and arms made out of sticks. We sacrificed Ge Ge's hat to put on his head.

As we admired the snowman, a thought hit me. Would the new baby grow up and play in the snow with us? By the time she became old enough to build a snowman, I would be in high school and Ge Ge would be desperately taking the SAT--basically the equivalent of *Gao Kao* here in America--to get into college. We probably wouldn't have time to play in the snow. Maybe he could play in the snow with Ming Ming.

BEEP! BEEP! That was Mr. Stevie.

"Come on, kids! First day of December! Hurry up and get to school so you can play in the snow!"

Even Mr. Stevie seemed cheerful. The snow certainly worked wonders on people!

On that first day of December, I sat with Olivia and Ivie on the bus. This snow seemed to be a fresh new start for everything.

After homeroom, Olivia, Ivie, and I headed to Chinese class. We walked slowly, talking and laughing and gushing about the snow.

Brrring!

Olivia gasped. "Oh no! That's the bell. Come on, Luolan, Ivie. Let's go!"

She took off. We raced after her, trying to keep up with her pace, gained from years of track practice, yelling things like, "Slow down!" "Can't . . . keep . . . up!" and "Olivia, you're gonna crash!" (This one because she was about to run into the Banana girl, aka Berecca Arlard.)

"Woah!" I stopped and looked up, out of breath from running. It was Ethan Arnold. With a girl next to him. "Hey, Luolan," he said. "What's up?"

"Not much." I glanced at the person beside him. It was Ellie Azalea. "Oh! Ellie. Hi!"

"Hey." Ellie looked uncomfortable. "Um . . . so . . . I take it you know Ethan?"

"Yeah, we're--" I broke off, not sure how to finish the sentence. Acquainted? In a situation? Together? "--friends," I managed.

"Yeah," Ethan nodded, looking relieved that I had saved him from explaining to Ellie. "So, you guys know each other. That's good. Ellie's my--"

Ellie cleared her throat pointedly, interrupting Ethan before he could say anything else. "Ahem! My class is starting soon. Bye, guys!" She dashed off. Smart.

Ethan awkwardly waved goodbye to me, then sauntered off. I didn't know how I felt. Annoyed? Mad? No. I felt *relieved*. I was only in sixth grade, after all. Better to let Ellie handle it with Ethan instead. And honestly, I had never been completely comfortable with the idea of Ethan in the first place.

Feeling like a huge weight had been lifted off my back, I turned and followed Ivie and Olivia to Chinese class.

* * *

I stuck around after class, waiting for everyone to file out. I had decided to tell Mrs. Henford about the email Rennie accidentally sent. She *was* my advisor, after all. She was supposed to help me with this kind of stuff.

"Uh, Mrs. Henford?" I asked. "Can I talk to you?"

She looked up from grading papers. "Oh, hi Luolan. Sure, come sit."

I pulled up a chair and sat down in front of her desk. "Can you read this?" I asked, giving her my iPad.

Mrs. Henford's lips moved silently as she read Rennie's email. Once she was finished, she looked up. "I think there's a story to be told here."

"Okay..." I cleared my throat. "Um, well..."

"From the beginning," she added.

So I did. I told her about moving from China, leaving my best friend, and the camping trip. I talked about accidentally telling Haiqing that I didn't want to be her friend anymore, and how Haiqing hadn't texted me since. When I finished, Mrs. Henford looked thoughtful.

"Seems to me you should be talking to your parents about this," she said.

I hesitated. "I know...It's just that my parents worked so hard to move here."

"So you don't want to tell them you're not having a good time here?" Mrs. Henford guessed. "Luolan, you should always tell your parents about these things, no matter what."

I must've still looked hesitant, because she added, "How about you just show them that email when you get home? You don't have to say anything, just let the words speak for themselves. Sound fair?"

"Okay." I nodded reluctantly. "Sure. But...Rennie *did* send email. Wouldn't it be...I dunno, rude to show it to Mother or Dad?"

"I'll talk to Rennie about it," Mrs. Henford promised. "Her, and I'll talk to her email pal's teacher. They shouldn't be talking about these things."

I nodded. "Thanks, Mrs. Henford."

She handed me a late pass. "You're welcome. Here you go." I took the pass. "Oh, and Luolan?"

"Yeah?"

"Don't worry so much. Just focus on making up with your friend."

"Okay."

"Now go, don't want to be even later for class!" She made a shooing motion with her hand. I laughed and ran off.

Skylar's Solution

I was expecting a huge lecture about friendship and saying mean things and stuff after I showed my parents the email, but Mama just folded her arms around me and Baba patted me on the back.

"I wish you'd told us about those things," Mama whispered. "I wish I'd known."

I was confused. "Aren't you guys mad at me about the fight?"

Baba shook his head. "No. We all make mistakes. It's how we go about making up for them that counts. We don't blame you, Luolan."

"Oh. But Haiqing--"

"I'll talk to her mother about it," Mama offered. "Then we can arrange something and--"

"No!" I cried. Then more calmly, "No. I want to make up with her myself."

Mama stared at me, the pride evident in her eyes. "*Ni zhang da le*, Luolan. You're growing up. I'm so proud of you." She hugged me tighter.

"Mama..." I muttered, squirming in her embrace. "Stop."

Baba chuckled.

Just then, Ge Ge came down the staircase. "Aww," he said. "What's happening?"

"Nothing!" I wriggled away from Mama and tore up the stairs and into my room, slamming the door in the process.

Behind me, I could hear Ge Ge saying, "And I thought *I* was fast!"

Just then, my phone *pinged*, signaling that I had mail. I opened the message and found that it was from Skylar. I read the message:

To: Luolan Xia

From: Skylar Byrne

Hey Luolan!

This morning I had a thought about our writing club poetry dilemma. Instead of just letting everyone write whatever they wanted, maybe they could all write short stories about their experiences with moving. It could be anything, poems, essays, opinion writing, I dunno, just please consider it. Feel free to add anything onto the idea and talk to me when we get back to school.

See you on Monday!

Sky

I felt honored. Skylar had asked *my* opinion? She must really value my decisions! I thought about her idea. It was good, I just didn't know if we had enough time for it. I typed a quick message back to her:

To: Skylar Byrne

From: Luolan Xia

Sky,

It's a good idea and I think we should do it, but I do not know if have enough time. We only have less than a month left, and we have to organize the festival. Let me know what you want to do.

Luolan

Her reply came almost instantly, but on my texts page:

Skylar: Maybe we could find a way 2 shorten it somehow?

Luolan: How?

Skylar: We could do it in groups, maybe that'll help, like each group do one thing

Luolan: do u wanna try it at meeting?

Skylar: Sure!

Luolan: 1 thing tho

Skylar: Yeah?

Luolan: I'm not being partners w/ Ethan

Skylar: Y?

Luolan: just cuz

Skylar: Got it. Gtg, going 2 park

Luolan: Bye

I put down my phone and sat back, flopping down on my pillows.

"Dinner," I heard Mama call, followed by Ge Ge and Ming Ming racing down the stairs. I smiled. I just couldn't wait for the meeting!

* * *

"Order!" Skylar was yelling, stomping her foot to call attention. "Order! What does a person have to do to get order in here?" She waved when she saw me come in. "Hey, Luolan!"

The room quieted a bit when I stepped through the door and came to stand at the front of the room. Skylar seized the moment. "Okay! So, Luolan and I had an idea about the project. We're still going to use Luolan's idea. But instead of just writing whatever you want about moving, we're switching it to a piece of writing about your experiences with moving.

"You don't have to have actually moved yourself. Maybe someone in your family moved, or maybe your friend is moving. That sort of thing. Oh, and by the way, we're doing it in groups. So each group only has to do one thing."

To my surprise, no one contradicted Sky's idea. Instead, everyone looked intrigued.

"So," she ventured, "is that a yes?"

Someone stood up. It was Ethan. "I'm in," he said, winking at me.

I rolled my eyes. So did he like me or Ellie? Did I care? Was he trying to get me into a competition with Ellie? Well, I didn't want to be in a competition with Ellie. It didn't matter anyway. I nodded at Ethan coolly and turned to everyone else.

"Anyone else?"

One by one, more people stood up. There were a few people I recognized: Abby Fergus-Falls, Ben Feindale, Adalie Falfale, and Hayley

Dellan from drama class, a few people that I didn't, and--oh gosh— **_Rennie? What was she doing here?_**

I didn't have time to think much about it, though. Skylar was already telling everyone to pair up. I dove to be partners with Adalie, but Hayley got to her first and they walked off together. Ethan and Ben paired up--not that I was going for either of them anyway--and Abby started off with a girl from her soccer team. Finally, there were only two people left: me and Rennie.

I glanced at Skylar desperately, trying to convey with my eyes that this was a bad choice.

"Um, Rennie--" she started to say, but Rennie cut her off.

"Come on, Ulan, let's go."

Adalie, Abby, and Hayley all glanced at me sympathetically.

"So..." I said awkwardly to Rennie, "I guess we're partners?"

"Yeah, I guess," she muttered.

"Where do you wanna sit?"

"I don't care."

"Oookay." I picked a random table and sat. "Here okay?"

"Sure."

"What do you wanna write about?"

"Stuff."

I gritted my teeth. She was making this so difficult! "So, should we write about your experiences or mine?" I asked, sure that she would say hers.

"Yours, I guess."

I thought I heard her wrong. From my experiences, Rennie *always* wanted to talk about herself. "Excuse me?"

"Yours," Rennie repeated, louder this time. "You've had way better experiences that I have had."

"What? Are you serious?"

"Yeah!"

I sighed. "I didn't know you were in writing club. When you get here anyway? And what happened to Cat?"

"She quit soccer practice," Rennie replied, making a face of disgust. "So, I did too."

"Why do you care what she's doing?"

"Just be quiet, okay?" Rennie snapped. "Let's just start."

"Okay..." I took out my pencil. "What kind of writing you want to do?"

It went like that for the rest of writing club. At the end of the hour, however, we'd put together a rough draft of what we were going to write. According to Rennie, I was supposed to take the draft and write the actual story myself. Great. She probably wanted to write about my experiences just so that I could do all the work and leave her with nothing to do.

I got on the late bus and sat in the back. Someone left a window open and it was freezing. I closed my window and sat back, shivering, my teeth chattering from the cold.

Someone slid in next to me. I looked over and caught a glimpse of Skylar's reddish golden brown hair.

"Hi, Sky," I said absentmindedly. She looked surprised.

"Since when did you start calling me Sky?" she asked.

"Oh!" I was surprised. I hadn't been paying attention to what I was saying. "Is that okay? I can stop."

"Oh no, it's fine. A lot of people call me that. I just never heard it come out of your mouth."

"New habit, I guess."

We laughed, our voices cut off when a cold gust of wind swept in from the window in front of us.

"Brrrr!" Sky chattered. "When did it get so cold?"

"It wasn't this cold this morning!" I agreed, jumping up to close the window. Rennie beat me to it.

"Oof!" we cried at the same time, bumping heads. "Ow! Why'd you do that?"

"I didn't do anything," Rennie replied, while I recoiled, rubbing my forehead.

"I was just closing the window," I told her, sitting down while she locked the window.

"So was I!" Rennie cried. "When *you* slammed into me!"

"To be fair, she didn't slam into anyone," Skylar tried to defend me. Rennie gave her a dirty look.

"Stay out of this, Byrne."

Skylar glared at her. "Calm down."

"You calm down!"

"No, you!"

"How 'bout we all calm down!" I shouted. By now, people were looking our way.

Sky and Rennie both sat down in a huff. I turned to Skylar. "You really didn't have to do that, you know."

"I know, but I've got a score to settle with Rennie."

I tilted my head. "What?"

Sky sighed. "It's a long story."

"I have time. My stop is the second-to-last."

"Okay." She hesitated. "I'll tell you."

The Story of Saoirse

"Not many people know this," Skylar began. "But my family immigrated from Ireland. My real name is Saoirse."

"Saoirse." It sounded cool in my mouth. *Ser-sha.* "That is such a pretty name! Why did you change it?"

"Because..." Sky trailed off, as if remembering bad memories. "Well, because I was ashamed. No one knew how to spell Saoirse and kids teased me about it. You see, my family immigrated here, but I didn't. Me and my little sister, Cara, were both born in the U.S. On the first day of first grade, when the teacher asked me what my name was, I replied, 'Skylar,' and that became my name forever."

"Was your mom upset?" I asked. I knew that Mama would be if I changed my name without telling her.

"No, actually," Sky replied. "She said that she had been planning on telling us to pick out new American names and was pleased I had already picked one out."

"Wow. But what happened for you to have score to settle with Rennie?" I asked, intrigued by her story.

"Rennie was mean to me from my first day of kindergarten onward," Skylar continued. "She teased me about my Irish heritage. She made fun of me and pulled my hair." Here, she paused and tugged at her coppery-brown hair herself. "I don't know why."

"She does the same to me, too," I replied. "Well, teasing anyway. Maybe she just has thing with people with different cultures than hers."

"I guess," Sky sighed. "I dunno. Anyway--me, I hated her. I swore revenge."

"Oh."

"Yeah. Pretty harsh. I never got through with it, though. Then, one day, when I was in fourth grade, there was a potluck supper for all the families on our street. Mom thought we should go, so while she baked some potatoes for us to take along, we put on our best clothes. Our whole family got in the car and drove to the supper. As we got out of our car, I saw another very familiar car pull up."

"Rennie?" I guessed.

"You got it. I can remember clearly that she was wearing a poofy yellow skirt that looked like an upside-down banana." She giggled, and I laughed, too. "I was wearing a blue dress with sequins all over the top and a matching headband. I was really proud of it, too."

"That sounds pretty." I trailed off, picturing how beautiful Skylar would look in a dress as lovely as she described.

"It was." Sky smiled. "I got out of the car, holding Cara's hand, doing my best to ignore her."

"Didn't work," I guessed.

"Obviously," she groaned. "I was spearing potatoes on a stick when Rennie came up to me. 'Hey, Skylar.' I thought she was going to say something nice, maybe compliment my dress or something, but instead, she said, 'I thought I would find you here. I mean, your family's from Ireland, right? And potatoes are Irish? So it makes sense that you would be eating them.'"

"That's mean!" I exclaimed. "What did you say?"

"I said, 'I'm eating potatoes because they taste good, not just because I'm Irish. Are you saying I should just sit around eating potatoes all day, not eating or doing anything else just because of my Irish heritage?'"

"Wow! What was her reply?"

Skylar's face darkened. "She replied, 'No. Wouldn't you be doing a jig or something?'"

"*What?* Why? That's . . . "

"I know, right? But this is the worst part: I couldn't take it anymore. I kicked her in the shin."

"What?" I wasn't sure whether to be shocked or happy for Sky. "Wow."

"Yeah. But you know what is so unfair? Instead of just kicking me back to get even, she kicked *Cara.*"

"Cara? Why?"

"I don't know! My sister didn't do anything to her! It was unfair and unjust and I've had a score to settle with Rennie this whole time."

"Until now," I added.

"Until now," Sky agreed. "You know, I feel bad for you, being stuck with her in the same grade."

"I feel bad for me, too."

"Luolan! Lizhong! Rennie! Come on! Don't straggle!" Mr. Stevie called. I looked out the window and realized the bus was at my stop. Time flew by while Skylar was telling her story.

"Bye, Sky," I said to her, calling her by my new nickname for her. "See tomorrow!"

"Yeah," she agreed cheerfully. "Tomorrow!"

I stood up and walked toward the front of the bus with my brother. As I passed Rennie's seat, though. I noticed something. Rennie had her ear pressed to the back of her seat, as if trying to hear the story Sky told about her. She clutched her backpack in one fist, her face turned toward the window.

But that didn't stop me from seeing her do something I hadn't thought she was capable of until now.

Rennie was crying.

Rennie Tells Her Story

I woke the next morning to a small *ping!* from my phone. I bolted upright and saw who the text was from: Haiqing. She wrote it in Chinese.

Breathless, I opened the text and read:

Haiqing:

Luolan,

I'm sorry for leaving you on the camping trip. I really missed you the last few months. I have something to tell you. Two somethings.

First: I'm so sorry that I haven't texted you. I couldn't figure out what to say.

Second: What I told you about Ziwei...a lot of it didn't happen. She's just a new girl in school who happened to play with me the first few weeks you were gone.

I told Mama and Baba about the fight. They said I can come to America to visit over summer break to make up for leaving the camping trip.

Please reply soon. Goodbye for now.

Your friend,
Haiqing Xu

I felt my heart being overcome with joy. Haiqing had forgiven me! And she was coming to America! To visit! I quickly typed up a message:

Luolan:

It's okay. Looking forward to seeing you!

-Luolan

"Hey! Luolan," Ge Ge called from downstairs. "You have a phone call!"

"Coming!" I scrambled up from my bed and raced downstairs. Who could it be? I never got phone calls.

In the kitchen, Ge Ge handed the phone to me. "Hello?" I asked.

"Hey, Luolan." I knew that voice. Rennie. And she actually said my name right.

"Rennie!" I tried to hide my surprise. "Um, I knew it was you all along!" Wait. No. What? That sounded weird. "Uh, hi! How are you?" There. Better.

"You need to listen to me," Rennie cried into the phone. "Please, just listen, okay?"

"Listen to what?"

"My story."

"Your story?" I was surprised. What did Rennie have to say? "Okay. Listening."

I plopped down on the couch in front of the TV where Ming Ming was watching dinosaurs beat each other to pieces. Not the greatest spot to listen to Rennie spill all her secrets, but at least no one would hear except Ming Ming who wouldn't understand any of it, anyway.

"You know how I've been, um . . . mean to you this whole school year?" Rennie began tentatively. "Accusing you of stuff and ganging up on you?"

"Believe me, I know." There was a tinge of sarcasm in my voice.

"I'm really sorry for that," Rennie continued. "And I'm really sorry for what I said to Skylar, too. I was just jealous of you."

"*You?*" I asked, disbelieving. *"Jealous?* But you have everything!"

"Not a cool culture like you," replied Rennie. "You have all those amazing foods and languages and traditions. I just have boring old Christmas and Thanksgiving."

"Those are great holidays, too," I reasoned.

"Maybe, but they're not...I dunno, special."

"I have a question," I said. "Why did you act like...like..."

"A spoiled brat?" Rennie asked, and I caught a faint smile in her voice. "I guess I just wanted attention. I thought that if I couldn't have a cool culture, then I should at least have people who pay attention to me."

We sat in silence for a while, me pondering what I'd just heard about Rennie, Rennie wondering if telling me had been a mistake. Finally, Rennie said, "So that's my story."

"Am I the only one who knows this?" I blurted. "Does anyone else know? Cat? Berecca?"

Rennie snorted. "Cat? She's such a copycat. Have you seen the way she dresses? It's like she's my twin! And I don't want a twin! If I told her my story, then she'd probably just copy me and tell me one of her long, boring stories about how she went to the ice cream shop and then found out that it was closed. And Berecca? She only cares about being the best."

I thought about saying, "Didn't you too, once?" but thought better of it. Instead I said, "So I'm the only one knows."

"Right."

"Don't worry. I will not tell."

"You'd better not. And Luolan?"

"Yeah?"

"I know what you're thinking. We can't be friends."

"W-what?" I was startled. What was she saying? I didn't want to be her friend! Or did I? Now that she had revealed who she really was inside, telling me her story and whatnot, maybe we could actually be good friends.

"We can't be friends. If we start being friends all of a sudden, then people will suspect that something's up. We can't be friends. I'm sorry, Luolan."

"But who cares if people suspect something's up?" I almost shouted. Ming Ming looked at me curiously, not understanding a word of what I was saying in English, but still sensing that something was wrong. I lowered my voice a little. "We can still be friends."

"No, Luolan. I'm really sorry."

"You should be!"

"But I won't tease you anymore. I can promise you that."

"You shouldn't tease anyone! It's mean!"

Silence. Then she spoke. "You're right."

"I know!"

"I won't tease people anymore."

"You shouldn't!"

"But I still can't be your friend."

"Why you care so much about what other people think?"

"Maybe someday, Luolan, but not now."

"Ugh." This wasn't right. But I could tell Rennie wasn't going to change her mind so I changed the subject. "Alright. Someday. That's a promise. You know, Rennie? You can be a pretty decent person when you aren't being a spoiled brat."

"Ha." Rennie laughed. "I have to go. Dentist appointment. See you tomorrow?"

"Yeah." I smiled and turned off the phone. Who thought I would ever say that to Renalda Ball?

The Writing Club Festival

"I can't find my tux" was the first thing I heard as I entered the gymnasium. It was the day of the Andrew Jackson Middle School Writing Club Festival and the gym was a mess. Ben Feindale was running around trying to find his missing tuxedo. Jamie Quinton had dropped his story and was on the floor, trying to grab it. Hayley Dellan and Abby Fergus-Falls were trying to set up their table while constantly getting harassed by Ben accusing them of stealing his tux.

"I'm telling you, we didn't steal it," Abby protested. "Why do you need a tux anyway? It's just a presentation."

She was wearing a green sweater and a jean skirt with her honey-colored hair braided down her back. Not very fancy, but any fancier and I knew Abby would explode. Hayley, on the other hand, wore a long dark blue skirt with sequins and a white blouse. She'd dyed her strawberry blonde hair with streaks of green for the occasion. Around her neck hung a sparkly H charm that looked like it was made of diamonds, but was probably just regular metal or plastic.

"Of course you did," Ben protested. "You stole my homework in fourth grade, *and* my baseball cap in third grade, *and* my favorite pencil in second! Why wouldn't you steal my tux now? And my dad got his

friend's son to lend it to me for free. He said I look very dignified in it."
He sniffed and looked down his nose at Hayley and Abby.

"Cody Davidson stole your homework in fourth grade, your sister
wore your baseball cap to school by accident in third, and you lost your
favorite pencil in second! You're just blaming Abby and me because
you hate us," Hayley protested. Then she sighed in exasperation and
pointed behind Ben. "There's your rented tux. Right there."

Ben turned. His tux was draped over the back of a chair in the corner
of the cafeteria. Ben turned bright red. "You--you!" he sputtered. "Ugh!
You two!" He stormed off, first to the corner of the cafeteria to get his
tux, then to the boys' restroom to change.

Both Hayley and Abby erupted in giggles. I looked at them in
surprise. "I thought you didn't do it!"

"We didn't," Hayley protested. "We just found it hanging on the
front door knob so we decided to put it where people could easily see
it."

"Yeah," Abby chimed in. "We had absolutely *no idea* it was Ben's."

"*None*," Hayley emphasized. "It just said "Property of Carson Levy"
on it and we knew there was no Carson Levy at this school, so we just
put it there. On the chair."

"Uh huh." I still wasn't a hundred percent sure that what they were
saying was true, but I decided to let it go. "You need finish setting up.
The festival will begin in few minutes."

"Got it." Hayley and Abby hurried to finish unfolding their table. I
moved on.

I just about checked everything and made sure everything was in
running order when Sky approached. "You do realize that the festival
is starting in two minutes, right?"

"It is?" I glanced at my watch. Sure enough, it was 3:58. The festival started at four. "But I still have six tables to check and--"

"Relax," Sky laughed. "I'm the writing club manager, remember? It's my job to check everything, not yours."

I blushed. "I know but--"

"Your partner's here."

"Oh." I glanced over at the other corner of the gym where Rennie was finishing setting up a table. "Great!" I sounded genuinely excited.

Skylar looked at me curiously. "Is everything okay?"

"Yeah. Everything is good. Gotta run!" I dashed off, leaving a very bewildered Sky probably wondering about my health.

"Hi, Rennie," I greeted her as soon as I reached the table. "You ready?"

"Shh, not so loud," she whispered. "I don't want anyone to see us talking!"

I rolled my eyes. Was she still trying to pretend we weren't friends? It had been a week and she still wouldn't talk to me in public! "We're partners, Rennie. We're supposed talk with each other."

The first two days had been a little tough. Rennie was at first a little embarrassed that she'd told me her story. Then, when I finally convinced her (not in public, of course) it was okay she had shared the story with me, she didn't speak to me for two more days.

Now we were speaking, but a bit edgy around each other. Rennie was still nervous to give me compliments. At least she had been friendly, though. She was probably just relieved she'd shared her story with someone. I wasn't going to take her friendship for granted, though.

"You look nice," Rennie said to me hesitantly.

I was wearing a pale pink dress with red Chinese-looking flowers embroidered around the edges. The dress was made of soft denim, the kind used to make jeans. (When I saw it in the store, I immediately whipped out my leftover money from my last babysitting job and purchased it. The dress was Chinese and American at the same time. Just like my family basically was right now.) For once, I didn't put my hair up in a ponytail, instead letting it cascade down my shoulders. I wore a red headband that matched my dress.

"Thanks! You look good, too!"

Rennie was wearing a dark purple dress that--in contrast--had light blue birds flitting around the neck, hem, and cuffs. Her curly brown hair was braided into two pigtails and tied together with a single purple ribbon.

"Thanks," she replied shyly. She probably wasn't used to taking compliments, either.

I draped our yellow-and-white checkered tablecloth over the table and set our story on it. Rennie and I stapled the pages together and I drew a picture for the cover. It showed an airplane flying between the two countries, America and China, with the words, 'Chinese-American: Luolan's Story of Immigration' on it.

Rennie opened our story and flipped through the pages. "It's really good," she told me. "You have a real talent for art and writing, Luolan."

There was no hesitation in her voice. I was flattered. "Thanks. You too."

"We're opening the doors soon!" Sky shouted over the noise. "Are you ready?"

"Yeah!" everyone yelled back.

"I said, _**are you ready**_?"

"**Yes**!" our writing club screamed.

"Okay! Oh, and after this, if you happen to have an idea for what our group name should be, then tell me," Skylar told us. Then she opened the doors.

The next few hours were a blur of people reading our story, complimenting Rennie and me, and saying what a good artist I was. At one point, Sky came up to Rennie and me. "There's this kid here. He wants you to read your story out loud."

"*What*?!" we chorused. "*Why*?!"

"I dunno, he just wants you to," Skylar said. She looked at us with large, pleading eyes. "Please? If you don't then he's gonna throw a tantrum and that's really bad for business."

Rennie and I glanced at each other. "Okay," we replied. "We'll do it."

Sky looked at the two of us questioningly. We really needed to tell her Rennie's story sometime.

"I'll do it," I volunteered.

"Are you sure?" Rennie asked. "I can do it if you want."

"No. My story. I'll do it."

"Oookay. If you're sure."

"I am." I looked at Sky. "Where I read?"

Sky led me to the little boy who had asked for me to read my story. He was standing with his parents, and when he saw me, he clapped hard.

"Are you the one dat moved to America from China?" he asked with large eyes, his thumb in his mouth.

"Yes," I replied with a smile. "I am."

"And you gonna read your story?"

"Mmhm."

"Now, Tim," the mother gently admonished her child. "You asked-- I'm sorry, I didn't quite catch your name," she said to me.

"Luolan," I told her.

"Right. You asked Luolan here to come read her story for you, so you have to listen."

"I do?"

The mom sighed. I got the feeling she went through this a lot. She turned to me. "Nice to meet you, by the way. My name is Paige Lopez. This is my son, Timothy, but he goes by Tim." She tilted her head. "By the way, do you, by any chance, know Mrs. Baker?"

I nodded. "Yes, I've babysat for Will before," I told her.

"Yes, Clara Baker told me about you," Mrs. Lopez agreed. She looked thoughtful. "I wonder, would you be willing to babysit Tim sometime? I'm always busy at meetings and things and my husband works full-time at the hospital.

"We always have to ask our neighbors to take care of Tim in the afternoons after he gets back from preschool and we feel bad about that because our neighbors have their own work to do. I'm not saying you have to, though. Only if you have time."

I thought for a moment. "For how long?"

"About two hours or so two times a week until we find someone else to take care of him. We'll pay you."

"Let me ask my parents, and I tell you."

"Great!"

"Excuse me?" Tim grumped, "You no read story anymore?"

"No, I'm still reading," I laughed. "I just talk to your mom about being babysitter."

"I don't need a babysitter," Tim proclaimed. "I'm a big boy now!"

"I'm sure." I sat down next to him. "Want me to read story?"

"Read story!"

I took that as a yes. I cleared my throat and opened the book.

My Story

It was a hot day, and a girl named Luolan and her friend Haiqing were sitting on the sofa in the living room slurping popsicles and staring out the window, watching cars go by. They were supposed to be doing their homework, but neither of them really felt like it. Luolan's homework lay in her lap, unfinished, and Haiqing hadn't even started hers.

"This interesting..." Tim murmured, interrupting me.

"Shh," Mrs. Lopez told him. "Listen to Luolan."

Luolan's mother was in the kitchen cooking up some delicious concoction for lunch, no doubt, and her father was taking Luolan's two brothers to a badminton game, so it was just Luolan and Haiqing in the living room. And that was how they liked it.

"I really think we should finish our homework," Luolan told Haiqing. "You know how Wang Lao Shi is about dilly-dallying."

"But we're not dilly-dallying," Haiqing protested. "We're just . . . enjoying this bright, sunny day!"

Luolan couldn't help but laugh and give in. The truth was that she didn't want to do her homework, either.

"If we're not going to do our homework, then what do you want to do?" Luolan asked Haiqing.

"Let's go play outside," she suggested.

Luolan agreed and soon they were both outside in the park, jumping rope and kicking a soccer ball around. Suddenly, Haiqing stopped the ball with her foot. "Hey, Luolan," she said. "Who is that?"

Luolan followed her finger. Haiqing was pointing to a tall boy with blond hair and glasses. He had his hands jammed into the pockets of his brown shorts and he wore a Red Sox baseball cap. He saw Luolan and Haiqing staring at him and waved.

Haiqing quickly dropped her finger. She hoped the boy hadn't taken offense of her pointing at him.

"Hey," the boy said, speaking Chinese with a slight accent. Luolan didn't recognize the accent, but she knew the Red Sox were an American baseball team. Could this boy be from America?

"Hi," both girls chorused, trying not to stare.

"I'm Spencer Lake," the boy with blond hair introduced himself. "You can call me Spen. Most everyone does."

"Spencer Lake," Luolan repeated, working the strange English words around her mouth. "Spen."

"My name is Xu Haiqing," Haiqing told him, remembering her manners. "Or Haiqing Xu, the American way."

"And my name is Luolan Xia," I added.

"Haiqing and Luolan," Spen repeated, just like Luolan had done with his name. "I like it. Do you live around here?"

Haiqing and Luolan nodded and he smiled. "Great! My family just moved here because of my dad's job. I'm in eighth grade."

"That's cool," they both managed.

Spen laughed. "At least you understand my terrible Chinese."

"No, no, it's not terrible," they replied hastily. It truly wasn't. He had gotten all the words right and his accent was almost perfect.

"Ha," Spen smiled. "Even my own sister says it's terrible. Her name is Kaylee, by the way. Kaylee Lake. She's in seventh grade. You'd like her."

"That's great."

By now, Spen had probably realized he was boring the girls. He caught sight of the soccer ball and grinned. "You play soccer?"

"No," Luolan told him. "I'm better at badminton."

"My favorite sport is swimming," Haiqing explained. "But soccer is great, too."

Spen smiled mischievously. Then he ran up to the ball, kicked, and sent it flying.

"Hey!" Haiqing shouted. Before she knew what she was doing, she had joined the game, kicking the ball out from between Spen's legs and dribbling it down the park.

Luolan laughed. She joined the game, too, racing after Haiqing and Spen. Haiqing passed the ball to her and she scored a "goal" between two rocks at the edge of the park.

"Not bad!" Spen called. The three flopped on the grass to take a break.

"So, what is America like?" Luolan asked Spen.

"Oh, not much different from here, actually," Spen told her. "It's loud and crowded and fun.

I moved here from St. Louis, Missouri. There's this structure there--it's called the St. Louis Gateway Arch. It's super cool. The first time my parents took me up there was when I was five and Kaylee was three. I remember I cried the whole way up."

They all laughed, Spen the hardest.

"I remember when I was four, Mama took me to this shopping mall to buy swim gear," Haiqing remembered. "She practically had to drag me up the escalator."

They all laughed and told stories until it was almost dark. Then Haiqing stood up. "I have to go," she sighed. "My mom wants me to help make dinner."

"Bye," Luolan and Spen said to her. Haiqing walked away. Then Luolan turned to Spen.

"What was moving to China like?" she demanded.

"Why?"

Luolan sighed. It was hard to get the words out. "Well . . . um . . . because . . . becausewemightbemovingtoAmerica," she said in a rush.

Spen blinked. "Excuse me?"

"Because we might be moving to America," Luolan repeated. "I heard my parents talking about it. And I'm scared. I don't want to go. At all."

"Oh." Spen looked thoughtful. "I know how that feels. Well, at first, moving feels really sad. You don't want to go, and when you arrive, you're pretty lonely."

"Thanks," Luolan grumbled. "Way to boost self-esteem."

Spen held up a hand. "Let me finish. But once you've stayed for a while, then it gets better. I promise."

Luolan's shoulders slumped. "I don't want to go," she whispered.

Spen nodded. "Who does?"

The two sat there for a few more minutes watching the sky slowly darken. Then, as the first stars began to show, the two departed and left for their homes.

The Last Big News

"You see him again?" Tim asked me, wide-eyed.

"See who?"

"Spencer Lake."

"No. I didn't. I wonder how he's doing now."

"Thank you so much for your time, Luolan," Mrs. Lopez said to me. "That was a beautiful story. You really do have a gift for writing."

I blushed. "Thanks."

"We'll be going now," Mrs. Lopez told me. "Come on, Tim."

As Mrs. Lopez and Tim walked away, I thought about Spen. I really hadn't seen him again. Was he still in China? Or had his father's job taken his family somewhere else? I never met his sister, Kaylee, who he said that I'd like. I wondered if he still knew me.

"Hey! Luolan!" Rennie called as she walked over. "How'd it go?"

"Pretty great, actually," I replied. "Tim was a great audience."

"Who?"

"Tim. The boy who I read my story to."

"Cool. Well, you'd better get back to our table. I have a spare copy, but it's photocopied. People want to see the real thing. Also, your family is waiting. They have news that they won't share with me."

I followed her back to the table. Ge Ge pulled me aside. "In front of the bathroom," he muttered. "Mama and Baba and Ming Ming are there already."

I followed him, puzzled, wondering what sort of "news" Mama and Baba had in mind. We couldn't be moving again, could we? Not when I had made so many new friends at Andrew Jackson Elementary!

"What's wrong?" I asked my brother.

Ge Ge shrugged. "Who knows? They won't tell me anything."

We walked all the way to the bathrooms in silence.

"Hey," I greeted my parents.

"Waby waby waby!" Ming Ming sang, jumping around on the floor and tripping over Baba's leather shoes.

I glanced at Ming Ming questioningly, wondering what he meant.

"What's the news you have?" I asked Mama, getting straight to business.

"Well..." Mama paused, building up the suspense.

"Come on come on come on!" Ge Ge squeaked, jittery all over. I felt the same way. What was happening? Why was Mama being so secretive?

"You know how we've been talking about having a baby?" Mama asked.

My heart beat faster. What? What was she getting at?

"Well, we went to the doctor today and..."

"C'mon, Mama, spill!" I pleaded.

"We're having a baby!"

"Oh my gosh!" I screeched, jumping up and down and forgetting that we were in a public space.

"Wow!" Ge Ge cried, picking Ming Ming up and twirling him around. *"Hao hao ya!* That's great!"

Baba laughed. "We knew that you kids would be super excited by that news." He made a dramatic voice. "A new addition to the Xia family!"

I laughed. "Is it a boy or a girl?"

"We don't officially know yet," Mama told me. "But I suspect that it's gonna be a girl." She grinned. "Mother's instincts."

"She predicted you were going to be a girl, Luolan," Baba said. "And that Ming Ming was going to be a boy."

"And I was right for both!" Mama declared proudly.

"You also predicted Lizhong was going to be a girl," Baba pointed out.

Ge Ge yelped. "***What***?"

We all laughed.

"I did," Mama admitted. *"Wo cuo la.* I was wrong."

"Obviously," Ge Ge declared.

Everyone laughed. We were all super excited about the new baby. But I was also excited by another thing: My life had finally calmed down.

I thought about my list of things I wanted to accomplish in America I made when we first arrived. 1. Make three new friends. 2.

Learn English. 3. Get people to like me. 4. Find a reason to call America 'home'. Yes. I had accomplished all of them. I had so many friends. I had a great--if still nameless--writing club. And I had Haiqing's visit to look forward to in the summer.

It was just like Spen said. After I'd stayed in America for a while, it actually wasn't so bad. Baba was right. It had truly been a once-in-a-lifetime experience.

But, once-in-a-lifetime experience or not, I liked my life better when it was normal. And it was now. Well, for the time being. The new baby was coming. And once it arrived . . . well, who knew what could happen then?

Epilogue

"Luolan?" Ge Ge called to me. It was Sunday and we were both eating ice cream in our rooms.

"Yeah?"

"Could you come over here?"

I exited my room and entered his. "What is it?"

Ge Ge was on his computer. He showed me his screen. "Look at this!"

"Massachusetts Annual Young Authors Contest," I read. "Entries of realistic fiction . . . sixth through twelfth grade . . . entered by the end of May...***Winner wins five hundred dollars???*** Oh my gosh, Ge Ge, this is amazing!"

"You should enter," Ge Ge told me. "You're a really good writer."

I smiled bashfully, happy that he was complimenting me. "I dunno. I probably wouldn't win, anyway. And the entry fee costs fifty dollars."

"So? You can earn the money from babysitting. And even if you don't win the whole contest, you can certainly win the sixth grade division and get one hundred dollars."

I grinned. "You think so?"

"Obviously! You're, like, the best writer in school!"

I knew he was exaggerating, but the comment made me feel great inside. Like a ball of fire slowly making its way through my body.

"But what if I don't win? Then that money would all be wasted."

"No, because you'll win."

"You're not gonna give up on this, are you?"

"No way. I'm not missing a chance to make my little sis famous. And take all the credit for it."

"You wouldn't dare!"

Ge Ge wiggled his eyebrows. "C'mon, Luolan."

I sighed.

"Please?"

"Alright." I sighed, smiling at the same time. "I'll enter."

The next few days I wrote and wrote and wrote. I finished just in time for the deadline. I printed my story out, folded it, and put it in an envelope. The envelope was almost bursting by the time I stuffed it in the mailbox.

I was absolutely certain this story was the best story I had ever written. Even if I didn't win, I would treasure it forever. It's the story of when I moved from China to America, after all.

Post-Epilogue

Dear Miss Luolan Xia,

We are pleased to inform you that you have won the Massachusetts Annual Young Writers Contest (MAYWC). The other judges and I greatly enjoyed your story about immigrating to America. We agree that you truly do have a future as a writer.

Enclosed with this letter is a MAYWC first place certificate, a check for five hundred dollars, and a gold medal. We hope that you continue to participate in MAYWC over the years to come. Congratulations!

Thank you for participating, and keep writing!

Signed,
Aya Mae Carson
Head Judge

Glossary of Mandarin Words and Phrases

(In order of appearance)

Tang hulu ....A type of Chinese candy
Xiao che .... Bus
Ni you xin! ....You have mail!
Fu..Chinese symbol for luck
Hao bang ya!..So great!
Ni zhang da le.. You're growing up
Hao hao ya! ....Wonderful!
Wo cuo la .... I was wrong

CPSIA information can be obtained
at www.ICGtesting.com
Printed in the USA
LVHW102016010422
715074LV00004B/108